OUT OF
THE MOUTHS
OF BABES

OUT OF THE MOUTHS OF BABES

SHELLEY KLEIN

MICHAEL O'MARA BOOKS LIMITED

First published in Great Britain in 2010 by
Michael O'Mara Books Limited
9 Lion Yard
Tremadoc Road
London SW4 7NQ

A CIP catalogue record for this book is available from the British Library.

Papers used by Michael O'Mara Books Limited are natural, recyclable products
made from wood grown in sustainable forests. The manufacturing processes
conform to the environmental regulations of the country of origin.

ISBN: 978-1-84317-480-6

1 3 5 7 9 10 8 6 4 2

www.mombooks.com

Cover design by Patrick Knowles

Text design and typesetting by Design 23

Illustrations courtesy of Jeannie Belle Davis (aged five and a half),
Frankie Dixon (aged nine) and Shante Bennett (aged six).

Printed and bound in Great Britain by CPI Cox & Wyman, Reading, RG1 8EX

CONTENTS

Grandma

ACKNOWLEDGEMENTS

A huge thank you to Gillian and Zoe Condon and to several friends and their respective children without whose help this book would have been all the more difficult. I am also extremely grateful to various friends and acquaintances who sent me the funny things their own darling children have said to them over the years, as well as the teachers who kindly took the time to ask their pupils a serious of daft-sounding questions for me. In addition I would like to credit all the wonderful publications and websites, too numerous to cite here but listed at the back of the book, which provided me with such a wealth of material as I researched this book.

INTRODUCTION

To see the world from a child's eye view is to see the world afresh. Nothing can prepare you for the funny, strange, charming – if slightly skewed – opinions and insights of those little people commonly known as children. If only we could all be as imaginative and (unintentionally) witty. But we can't, and therein lies the charm of listening to those who are younger, and less well versed in the ways of the world, than us. After all who but a child would say, with some certainty, that God lives in a big coconut? Or would say that when they grow up they want to be a 'dinosaur doctor'?

When asked to identify the worst thing about being a child, Henry, aged five (and a half), piped up, 'Mum keeps sticking me in the bath. I mean, I only have to look at a worm or a puddle and next second I'm in the bath.' Poor Henry! Life's tough when you're small: there are so many demands on you and so much stuff to work out about the world. Indeed, some of the best jokes and anecdotes in this collection are on this subject alone. But getting things slightly muddled or completely wrong is one of the prerogatives, if not the charm, of childhood. Take the following exchange between the presenter Art Linkletter and a young guest on his show:

Kid: My father's a nurseryman and raises flowers.

Linkletter: What sort?

Kid: Algerians.

Linkletter: Algerians?

Kid: Yes, red ones, white ones, pink ones.

Linkletter: Don't you mean geraniums?

Kid: Yes, Algerians.

Linkletter interviewed thousands of children for his then ground-breaking US radio and TV show *Party House*, excerpts of which were anthologized in a book called *Kids Say the Darndest Things*. Later the wonderful and extremely funny Bill Cosby took over Linkletter's mantel by interviewing an equal number of children for his TV series *Kids Say the Darndest Things*, which in turn inspired *Kids Say the Funniest Things* in the UK, hosted by Michael Barrymore. I am deeply indebted to all of these shows and their respective books, as well as to several wonderful stories which first appeared in *Little Gems*, *Babes and Sucklings*, *Pass the Port* and the subsequent volume *Pass the Port Again*, as well as quotes and letters from children from numerous publications, including the wonderful books *Butterfly Kisses*, *Dear God*, *What Religion Were the Dinosaurs?*, *Children's Letters to God* and *Children's Letters to Santa Claus*.

That there are so many examples of those unpredictable and unintentionally hilarious things children say to be found out there only goes to prove how refreshing and amusing our little treasures can be (apart, of course, from when they're your *own* little treasure and behaving like a little monster). Indeed I would be so bold as to say that seeing things from a child's point of view is one of the most thought-provoking things you can do. Logic is turned on its head, the norm is no longer normal: when a friend's child was asked what her favourite colour was, the answer came back 'rainbow'. What a wonderful answer – one that very few (if any) grown-ups would have thought of, but that makes absolute sense. This book is crammed with similar – strangely wise – little jewels, so, whether quoted straight from the mouths of our children, or told in the form of jokes and stories, if you are in need of a good chuckle or a new way of seeing the world, you really could do no better than pick up a copy of *Out of the Mouths of Babes* and let yourself be thoroughly entertained.

SHELLEY KLEIN, 2010

OFF TO SCHOOL

my teacher

It can be a heart-wrenching day sending your beloved child off for their first day at school; resplendent in their oversized uniform (they'll grow into it soon enough), clutching their packed lunch in excited expectation and, of course, blissfully unaware of their parents' worries as they skip off to make new friends and learn new things. Some of the best anecdotes and most hilarious quotes in this collection have come from teachers, parents and school kids; the classroom and the playground are, after all, where kids' imaginations are given free reign, with often very funny and touching results.

SWIMMING CERTIFICATE

Three-year-old Charlotte was in raptures after being given a certificate of achievement in her swimming lesson. When her father came home from work that evening, Charlotte's mother proudly handed him the award.

'Charlotte, are you going to tell Daddy what this is?' she prompted.

'Daddy,' she said, beaming with pride, 'this is my terrificate!'

PLAYING GAMES

A father had taken his son Ben to the dentist one morning before dropping him off at school. When they arrived at the school office to sign him in, they overheard one of the secretaries talking to the headmaster about two girls who had been caught 'playing hooky'. Ben immediately turned to his Dad. 'Dad, Dad,' he whispered, 'how do you play hooky? It sounds like a fun game!'

SHORT AND TO THE POINT

This charming story within a story is related in the collection *Pass the Port*. One day a teacher asked the class to write a story containing the following four elements: romance, mystery, royalty and religion. One little boy, who clearly understood the beauty of brevity, got the job done in thirty seconds. On being asked by his teacher to share his creation with the rest of the class, he promptly read out:

' "God!" said the Duchess. "I'm pregnant."

"Oo done it?" asked the butler.

The End.'

Teacher: Harriet, please go and stand by the map and point out America.

Harriet (pointing to the correct continent): This is America, Miss.

Teacher: Very good, Harriet. Now, class, who discovered America?

Class: Harriet, Miss.

DEAD AS A . . .

In a junior school assembly one day a headmistress announced that each child was going to be given a form that they should take home to be signed by their parents and returned to their form teacher. 'The deadline,' the headmistress said, 'is Friday.'

One little girl dutifully took the form home in her school bag and asked her mother to sign it. 'Mum, on Friday there's going to be a dead lion in school. Why do you think there's going to be a dead lion there on Friday?'

I like my teacher because she likes Star Wars and Doctor Who. One day we're going to dress up as Daleks together.
Sidney — aged eight

SHOW AND TELL

Children can cause so much trouble without even trying . . . When collecting her daughter from nursery school, a mother found out that the topic of a 'Show and Tell' that day had been parents' occupations. The teacher of the class took the little girl's mother to one side to warn her that she should perhaps explain a bit more about her job to her young daughter. The mother replied that she was a training consultant and travelled with her job, leading seminars in hotel conference rooms.

'Oh, I see,' said the teacher. 'It's just that your daughter told the class she wasn't sure what you did, but you dressed very prettily and went to work in motels.'

IS IT A PLANE? IS IT A BIRD? NO . . .

A professor of humanities at St Andrews University told an anecdote in *Pass the Port Again* about a primary school drawing class near his home. The teacher asked the class to draw a picture of 'The Flight into Egypt'. Some imaginative pieces of artwork followed. One memorably featured a Mary, Joseph and Jesus on board a Boeing 707. There was also a mysterious figure at the front of the plane.

'Who's that?' asked the teacher.

'Oh,' said the child, 'that's Pontius the Pilot.'

WHAT DO YOU KNOW, DAD?

One father from Shropshire wrote into *The Times* letter pages, telling of how his efforts to help his ten-year-old daughter with her maths homework were met with 'What do you know about it, Dad?' When he replied that he actually had a degree in maths, he was roundly dismissed: 'Well, you couldn't get one now.'

Teacher (to the class): How can we prevent the spread of nasty diseases caused by biting insects?

Mark, aged six: Don't bite any?

YOU WERE WARNED

Spotting that one of her young pupils was making faces at the other children in the playground, Miss Asper took little Keith aside. 'Keith, when I was a child we were told that if we made ugly faces and the wind blew then our face would stay that way.'

'Well, Miss,' replied the boy, 'you can't say you weren't warned.'

COULD DO BETTER?

On leaving his first post a teacher received a card from his class which read: 'Thank you for learning us so well'. Never being quite sure if the writers of the card were joking or if the mistake was genuine, he nonetheless treasured the first two words.

Question to Jack, aged eleven: What would you like to give up for Lent?

Jack: School.

HOW EXTREMELY OBSERVANT

An eminent professor of statistics submitted this anecdote to *Pass the Port*. He once took his young son and daughter to an evening for children at Harvard University Observatory. Unfortunately a cloudy sky meant that, apart from a fleeting view of the moon, the powerful telescopes showed nothing. As a result, the children (mostly under ten but extremely precocious) and their doting parents were instead given a talk by a bright young astronomer. The talk was on 'Sizes of Heavenly Bodies' and as the astronomer spoke, using the prop of a huge balloon, over a hundred tiny hands scribbled down pencilled notes.

At the end of the talk, the lecturer opened the floor to questions. The first hand shot up and a seven-year-old boy read out a carefully prepared question from a slip of paper.

'Will the lecturer please tell us how far it is from the Earth to the planet Mercury?'

'It depends,' the lecturer said, unwilling to commit to an exact figure, 'on the time.'

'Well, say at six-thirty?'

Dear God,
We read Thomas Edison made light. But in school they taught us that you did. So I bet Edison stoled your idea.
Sincerely,
    Donna (age 7)

MOTHER LOVE

A mother dropped her son off for his first day at primary school. She was very proud of him in his brand new school uniform and at the gate she kissed and hugged him over and over again. 'Darling, be a good little bunnikins for your mother. Mummy loves her baby boy very much.'

At the end of the school day the little boy came out of the school gates to find his mother waiting, arms open wide for a big hug. 'And what did my little soldier learn today?' she asked.

'I learned,' replied her son very seriously, 'that my name is David.'

Teacher: Why are you late again, Sam?

Sam: Because of the sign.

Teacher: What sign?

Sam: The sign that says 'Children, Go Slow'.

PICK UP A PENGUIN

The American humorist James Thurber once related a very sweet little story about a teacher who gave her class a book on penguins to read, after which they were asked to write an essay on it. One little girl, apparently unimpressed, wrote an essay that consisted of a single sentence: 'This book told me more about penguins than I wanted to know.'

Teacher to Michael, aged eight: Michael, what is the chemical formula for water?

Michael: H, I, J, K, L, M, N, O.

Teacher: What on earth do you mean?

Michael: Miss, you told us yesterday it was H to O.

SICK NOTES

While working as a primary school teacher in Canada, Karen Franklin's pupils would occasionally bring her a letter from their parents explaining why they had been absent the previous day. One little boy brought her a note, which he had very obviously written himself, saying: 'John was not in school yesterday afternoon because his rat was ill and he had to stay home and rub its tummy.'

PARLIAMENTARY QUESTION TIME

This little anecdote was told by a former Clerk of the House of Commons in the wonderful collection *Pass the Port Again*. He first explains how public petitions submitted by Members of Parliament are placed in a green cloth bag that hangs on the back of the Speaker's Chair in the House of Commons.

Normally the petitions are extremely long and detailed. However, one night many years ago, after a party of schoolchildren had visited Parliament and been escorted through the lobbies, a messenger brought the Clerk a scrap of paper which had been found in the bottom of the bag. It simply read: 'Wot about school dinners?'

TEACHERS LIVE AT SCHOOL

Carol Smith's story shows how some teachers are sadly taken for granted. Her six-year-old son came home after his first day back at school following the long summer break. Carol asked him what his classmates had done over the holidays: they had been camping, going to water parks, visiting the zoo, visiting Granny, having holidays abroad . . . 'And what did Miss Shipley do?'

'Nothing, she just sat in the classroom and waited for us all to come back.'

TO BE OR NOT TO BE

The school play is often an unintentional cause for hilarity as the following anecdote from *Pass the Port Again* testifies. A young boy at boarding school wrote to his mother and father about the school play in which he had had a role, but which they had unfortunately missed. 'The play,' he wrote, 'was *Hamlet*. Most of the parents had seen it before, but they laughed just the same.'

WHY ARE TEACHERS ALWAYS OLD?

The following is a little story from a primary school teacher called Isabel who was celebrating her twenty-eighth birthday one day with some of the children from her class.

After singing 'Happy Birthday' to her, the class grew quiet, until one little girl plucked up the courage to ask her a question: 'Miss, how old are you?'

Isabel replied, tongue-in-cheek, that she had just turned fifty.

'Wow,' said the little girl. 'And you're still alive!'

Teacher: If I had ten oranges in one hand and eight oranges in the other, what would I have?

Charlie: Big hands!

CHICKEN LITTLE

A primary school teacher was reading the story *Chicken Little* to her pupils when she came to the part when our hero, Chicken Little, warns the old farmer that the sky is falling in. The teacher continued, 'And so Chicken Little tried to warn the farmer and said, "The sky is falling, the sky is falling!"'

The teacher then paused and asked her pupils, 'And what do you think the farmer said?'

A little boy raised his hand, 'Please, Miss, the farmer said, "Holy mackerel! A talking chicken!"'

Teacher: Stop acting the fool, Jones.

Jones: I'm not acting, sir!

WHO'D BE A TEACHER?

The following classic story appeared in *Pass the Port Again* and tells of a young, eager teacher who was giving a lesson on the metric system. She explained carefully the various measurements – millimetres, centimetres, metres, kilometres, grams, kilograms, litres etc. At the end of the lesson she then had the bright idea of asking her pupils to compose a sentence each using one of the metric terms, to show that they had fully understood what they'd been taught. To one little boy the teacher said, 'Tommy, give me a sentence with the word centimetre in it.'

Tommy pondered for a moment, then said, 'Miss, my grandma came to see us last night and I was sent to meet her from the station.'

WHO ARE YOU?

As a boy, the renowned Shakespearean actor Laurence Olivier was already showing signs of greatness in a school production of the bard's *Julius Caesar*. The ten-year-old boy was spotted by a famous actress, Ellen Terry, who had been persuaded to come and see the play by the school's ambitious headmaster. 'The boy who plays Brutus is already a great actor,' announced Terry after the play was over. However, when this praise was relayed to the young Olivier he replied, 'Yes, but who is Ellen Terry?'

The process of filtration makes water safer for drinking because it removes large pollutants like grit, sand, dead sheep and canoeists.
        Kevin — aged nine

I'M GOING TO GRACELAND

A secondary school teacher was teaching a class about Ancient Greece when she asked if anyone knew where Greece was before looking it up on a map. One bright spark answered, 'Yes! Isn't that where Elvis lives?'

DEAR DIARY

This example of the misinterpretation of adults appeared in Gervase Phinn's book *Little Gems*. Richard, aged six, wrote in his school diary: 'Last night my daddy beat my mummy again.' His mother had to explain to his concerned form teacher after school that she had, in fact, been beaten at Scrabble.

Pupil: Miss, would you punish someone for something they hadn't done?

Teacher: No, of course I wouldn't.

Pupil: Good, then you won't mind that I haven't done my homework.

NAUGHTY, NAUGHTY!

This conversation was once overheard by a teacher at an end-of-term disco, as a boy approached one of the older girls:

'The headmaster is such an idiot, isn't he?' said a boy to a girl in the year above.

'No,' the girl answered. Pause. 'Do you know who I am?'

The boy admitted that he didn't.

'I'm the headmaster's daughter,' she said haughtily.

'And do you know who I am?' asked the boy.

'No.'

'Thank goodness!' said the boy, sidling off with a huge sigh of relief.

Pip: Mum, I can't go to school today.

Mum: Why not?

Pip: I don't feel well.

Mum: Where don't you feel well, Pip?

Pip: In school.

DREAMY

An eight-year-old boy once approached his form teacher in the school canteen with a worried expression on his face. 'Mrs Adams,' he said, 'I had a dream about you last night.'

'Did you?' Mrs Adams said with surprise. 'What was the dream about?'

'I can't tell you,' he said.

'Why not?' Mrs Adams asked. 'Was I shouting at you?'

'No,' he said in a whisper. 'You didn't have any clothes on!'

THE MAN IN THE MOON

Sir Robert Cockburn tells a story, which appears in *Pass the Port Again*, of a teacher who was one day telling her class all about the Apollo moon landings. All her pupils were very attentive but one little boy was already an avid reader about space travel, and as a result kept interrupting the teacher to correct her.

'The astronauts,' said the teacher, 'took off from Cape Canaveral . . .'

'No, Miss, they blasted off.'

'Then,' she continued, 'they flew off to the moon.'

'No, they didn't – they went into orbit.'

'And when they landed . . .'

Again the boy interrupted, 'Miss, it's only the lunar module that sets down on the moon's surface.'

Finally the teacher finished the lesson and dismissed the class with an enormous sense of relief. However, when all the other children had left the classroom she noticed the little boy had stayed behind.

'Miss,' he said, 'Father Christmas does still live on the moon, doesn't he?'

WHERE'S FELIXSTOWE?

A little girl with a classmate called Felix came home one day and relayed this exchange to her mother. Their teacher had asked the class, 'Where is Felixstowe?' And one child put his hand up to reply, 'On the end of Felix's foot.'

DICTATION

Mrs Cluley related a story about her ten-year-old son's music lesson in Nigel Rees's *Babes and Sucklings*. The teacher dictated to the class, 'His sighs grew with his ardour.' Her son was extremely puzzled and asked: 'Is that spelt S-I-Z-E, Sir?'

Teacher: Simon, your homework on 'My Dog' was very interesting. But your brother wrote exactly the same thing. Did you copy it off him?

Simon: No, Miss, it's just the same dog.

Some teachers are lovely but some teachers look like Frankenstein.
Charlotte — aged seven

THE SCHOOL REPORT

At the end of every school year children all over the country have to take home their school reports for their parents to read. Quite apart from the marks inside, the main aim, from the child's point of view at least, is to present the contents of said report in the most flattering possible light. In this subject, at least, the following pupil obviously scored A+:

'Hello Dad! Do you realize what a lucky father you are?'

'No, Tom. And why is that?'

'Well, you don't need to buy me a whole new set of textbooks for next year, because I'll be in the same class again. Brilliant, isn't it?'

Teachers are there to annoy us, but they deserve higher pay anyway. They are captured and tortured until they agree to be a teacher.
Max — aged nine

LUNCH MONEY

A head teacher at a primary school once received the following note from a concerned parent, which later appeared in the collection *Pass the Port Again*:

'Dear Head Teacher,

Robert has swallowed a 50 pence piece. I am keeping him in bed but will be calling in the doctor if there is no change by Monday.'

Teacher: Joe, how do you get so dirty so quickly?

Joe: I'm a lot closer to the ground than you are, Miss.

TOP MARKS

Many moons ago, when the Eleven Plus exam was still taken by schoolchildren across the country, an examiner recalls in *Babes and Sucklings* how he was once marking some papers which included a section testing vocabulary. In one of the questions, the children were asked to write down a word to describe 'a man who keeps on despite all the difficulties'. One girl had written down:

'Passionate.'

ON BEING FRUGAL

A New Zealand teacher, hopeful of expanding her pupils' vocabulary, gave her class a list of new words and asked them to write a short paragraph using each word, in order to demonstrate they had understood its meaning. One of the words on the list was 'frugal' – which one small boy obviously knew had something to do with saving. The boy wrote the following: 'A beautiful princess was at the top of a tall tower, where she was kept prisoner by an evil troll. She saw a handsome prince riding by. "Frugal me, frugal me," cried the beautiful princess. So the handsome prince climbed the tall tower and he frugalled her and they lived happily ever after.'

Teachers smell nice but they get in bad moods and stamp their feet when they're very cross.
   Chris – aged eight

LOVE IS . . .

Love is a big word, but for kids it can be applied indiscriminately to Mum, the cat or raspberry ripple ice cream. Children have the most endearing and funny ways of expressing their love – for one little boy the best person to kiss is his mummy – and most of this chapter is in the form of quotes from children themselves. But kids can sometimes see the adult world of relationships with piercing clarity too, such as the child who declared that love is 'when Daddy offers to do the washing up' . . . And it probably is.

No one is sure why people fall in love, but I heard it has something to do with how you smell. That's why perfume and deodorant are so popular.
Mae, aged nine

RETAIL THERAPY

When Karen, aged six, was asked if she had ever been in love, she clearly felt under pressure to justify her answer in some way, even if she had only a vague notion of what 'love' might be: 'No,' she replied, and then added brightly, 'but I've been shopping this morning with mummy.'

If you want to be loved by somebody who isn't already in your family, it's very helpful to be beautiful.
Anna — aged nine

Wait and see if the man pays for the meal. That's when you can tell if he's really in love.
Bobby — aged nine

WHAT IS LOVE?

A tough question even for adults – and it has given rise to some sweet, surprising and funny responses from kids everywhere. Emily, aged eight, responded, 'Love is when you kiss all the time. Then when you get tired of kissing, you still want to be together and you talk more. My mummy and daddy are like that. They look gross when they kiss.' Alan, aged five, said hopefully, 'Love is when Daddy says I can have a kitten. He hasn't said it yet, but I know he will because he loves me.'

Meanwhile, Martha, aged nine, has the realities down pat: 'Love is when Mum tells Dad he can go to the football and she doesn't pull a face.' Although perhaps not as accurately as Mark, aged six, who said 'Love is when Mummy sees Daddy on the toilet and she doesn't think it's disgusting.'

Question to six-year-old boy: If you were married how would you make sure your wife always felt happy?

Boy: Tell her she was very beautiful even if she looked like a gorilla!

TRUE LOVE IS A PEDICURE

When one little boy was asked about the nature of true love he explained that his granny had recently developed arthritis and couldn't bend over far enough to paint her toenails any more (clearly a glamorous gran). 'So my granddad does it for her now, even though he's got arthritis too. That's love.'

When you love somebody your eyelashes go up and down and little stars come out of you.
   Karen — aged seven

Most men are brainless, so you might have to try more than once to find a live one.
   Angie — aged ten

I bet it's very hard for God to love all the people in the world. There are only four people in my family and I can never do it.
   George — aged six

Question to David, aged ten: How do you decide who to marry?

David: You got to find somebody who likes the same things. Like if you like football, she should like it that you like football and she should keep giving you crisps and cans of beer.

I know one reason kissing was invented. It makes you feel warm all over, and in the olden days they didn't always have electric heat or fireplaces in their houses.
    Gina — aged eight

It's never OK to kiss boys. They always slobber all over you. That's why I stopped doing it.
    Tammy — aged ten

Romantic adults usually are all dressed up, so if they are just wearing jeans, it might mean they used to go out or they just broke up.
    Sarah — aged nine

Question to Pam, aged seven: When is it okay to kiss someone?

Pam: When they're rich.

I'm not rushing into being in love. I'm finding year six hard enough.
  Regina — aged ten

KISS CHASE

Jamie, at the tender age of six, complained to his mum that he was being hounded by a group of girls trying to kiss him and saying they wanted to marry him. He eventually told them to stop and stood his ground, saying sternly, 'Oh no, I cannot kiss or get married until I have a moustache and a beard.'

The best person to kiss is your mummy.
  Schoolchild, Woking

When a man and a woman get married they promise to go through sickness and illness and diseases together.
  Marlon — aged ten

Dates are for having fun and people should use them to get to know each other. Even boys have something to say if you listen long enough.
Lynne — aged nine

My mother says the best thing she did was get married. It was the happiest day of her life except when I was born, though it did hurt a bit.
Andrew — aged eleven

When you're in love you get to go to cafés with your boyfriend.
Schoolchild, Woking

FRIENDSHIP, POSSIBLY MORE

When asked what exactly marriage was, Anita, aged nine, gave it some serious thought. She decided that a boy proposes after he and his girlfriend have been going out a while, before adding, 'And then he says to her, "I'll take you for a whole lifetime, or at least until we have children and get divorced, but you have to do one particular thing for me." And then she says, "Yes", but she's wondering what the thing is and whether it's naughty or not. She can't wait to find out.'

We all love everyone in our family — except for my brother. I don't love him very much, but you can't love everyone, can you?

Harriet — aged nine

I have five boyfriends; three are older than me but two are younger. They're still in nursery school so they don't know how to kiss properly yet.

Gemma — aged seven

Question to Michelle, aged nine: What are most people thinking when they say 'I love you'?

Michelle: The person is thinking, 'Yeah, I really do love him, but I hope he showers at least once a day.'

When you get married you have to find someone who likes sleeping in the same bed as you. Of course, you have to buy a big bed. At the moment my bed is too small for me to get married.

Thomas — aged six

MANKILLER

The following is an excerpt from the Art Linkletter's TV show *House Party*. Here the Linkletter is interviewing a very candid (and very popular) seven-year-old little girl.

Linkletter: What is love?

Girl: When you're at school and someone chases you.

Linkletter: But suppose you're being chased just for fun.

Girl: Oh, that's love, not fun.

Linkletter: But don't you get chased by lots of different boys?

Girl: Yeah, all the ones that love me.

Linkletter: About how many, would you say?

Girl: I never stopped to count them, but lots.

Linkletter: Is that the best thing about school?

Girl: Well, lunch is good too.

Married people usually look happy to talk to other people.

    Eddie — aged six

You can tell if two people are in love because they stare at each other for ever and ever and ever . . .

    Schoolchild, Woking

Question to Billie, aged eight: Will you sleep in the same bed as your wife when you get married?

Billie: I might sleep in the same bed but we won't kiss because that's disgusting.

Question to Joby, aged five: How can you tell who to marry?

Joby: By seeing how much money they give you for your birthday.

ENDLESS LOVE

Kids can often have the most charming and disarming views on love, and often seem to get closer to the truth than people supposedly older and wiser than themselves. When Carolyn, aged eight, was asked what was the best age to get married she replied, 'Eighty-two! Because by then you won't have to work any more, and you can spend all your time loving each other in your bedroom.'

Question to Manuel, aged eight: How do you fall in love?

Manuel: You get shot with an arrow or something, but the rest of it isn't supposed to be painful.

If falling in love is anything like learning how to spell, I don't want to do it. It takes too long.
     Glenn — aged seven

Love will find you, even if you are trying to hide from it. I have been trying to hide from it since I was five, but the girls keep finding me.
     Bobby — aged eight

Love is when you go to McDonald's and give somebody most of your chips without making them give you any of theirs.
     Bella — aged six

No person really decides before they grow up who they are going to marry. God decides it all way before, and you get to find out later who you're stuck with.
    Karen — aged ten

If you're in love don't do things like have smelly, green sneakers. You might get attention, but attention isn't the same thing as love.
    Alonzo — aged nine

HOME HELP

Amy was a bright, sweet, inquisitive child. One day while she was talking with her father she confessed that she didn't really understand what marriage meant so her father went and fetched the wedding photo album and went through it with her, explaining the ceremony, the vows that were taken, the party afterwards, the cutting of the cake, and so on. At the end of the album he turned to his daughter and said, 'Now do you understand?'

'I think so,' said Amy. 'Is that when Mummy came to work for us?'

Love is when a girl puts on perfume and a boy puts on aftershave and they go out and smell each other.
    Karl — aged five

Falling in love is like an avalanche where you have to run for your life!
 John — aged nine

When you marry people, you actually have to kiss them.
    Naomi — aged six

The real problem is that girlfriends aren't like pets. You can't just go in to a shop and choose one. You have to take girls out to the cinema.
    Leon — aged seven

Question to Gracie, aged six: What do most people do on a date?

Gracie: They go out for dinner, after that I think they have kids.

TOUGH LOVE

Kurtis, aged five, was a contestant on Michael Barrymore's *Kids Say the Funniest Things*. When asked by Barrymore about his love-life, he replied calmly, 'I've got four girlfriends. One said she loves me and that I had to turn around, the next one started shouting at me, and the third one keeps on trying to carry me and make me sit on her. And the fourth one doesn't really like me.'

It's love if they order one of those desserts that are on fire. They like to order those because it's just like how their hearts are — on fire!
    Christine — aged nine

Question to Craig, aged nine: What would you do on a first date that was going badly?

Craig: I'd run home and play dead. The next day I would call all the newspapers and make sure they wrote about me in all the dead columns.

I know my sister loves me because she gives me all her old clothes and then has to go out and buy new ones.
Lauren — aged four

You have to be good at kissing so that your wife forgets that you never take out the recycling.
James — aged ten

I want to have a girlfriend for fifty years. No, make that fifty-one years.
Schoolchild, Woking

Question to Derrick, aged eight: How can a stranger tell if two people are married?

Derrick: You might have to guess based on whether they seem to be shouting at the same kids.

SOB STORY

Children are immune to the daft sentimentality that affects adults. When asked what she thought the big deal about 'love' was, ten-year-old Lizzie replied, with a grimace, 'Well, it makes everyone get the tissues out when there is a big smooch at the end of a sad movie, but I think it is nice until tongues get involved.'

FAMILY MATTERS

Mothers, brothers, sisters, fathers, aunts, uncles, grannies and grandpas – no one can escape the piercing gaze of the youngest of the family. Whether it's letting the cat out of the bag about Auntie's hairy arms or asking Granny whether she was on Noah's Ark, kids have a knack of bringing comic relief to any family (when they're not causing mayhem) as the following anecdotes and quotes will testify.

GRAVE THEORIES

A mother overheard her two daughters discussing the house owned by their grandmother, which has a cemetery running along one side of the house and garden. The eldest, eleven, said that she couldn't see why their grandmother would want to live so close to it. The youngest daughter, nine, piped up, 'Oh, well, it's probably because when she dies, they won't have far to take her.'

God made mummies to keep the houses clean. He made daddies to tell mummies to keep the houses clean.
   Alistair — aged five

Dear God,
please send some clothes for those poor ladies in Daddy's magazines.
   Louisa — aged six

A SILLY STORY

Alfie, aged seven, was asked by his sister to be a pageboy at her wedding. Very excitedly, as he was walking down the aisle he began taking two steps, then turning to the guests on either side he would put up his hands like claws and begin roaring. And so it continued; step, step, 'ROAR,' step, step, 'ROAR,' all the way up to the altar. The wedding guests found this extremely funny and howled with laughter but Alfie didn't think it was a laughing matter at all and by the time he reached his sister was almost in tears.

'Why are they laughing at me?' he said wiping his eyes.

'Well, what were you doing when you came down the aisle?' whispered his sister.

'I was being the Ring Bear, of course!'

Dear God
Now that I am ten I want to have a talk with you, please. I am just about a hole [sic] decade. And you may not believe this, but I have never been water skiing. I think it is Time. Tell my dad to loosen up.
    Cheryl — aged ten

Dear God
Maybe Cain and Abel would not have killed each other if they had their own rooms. That's what my mum did for me and my brother.
    Ali — aged seven

NOT SO LOUD NEXT TIME!

Sometimes children's voices carry much further than you would rather, as in this anecdote told by an embarrassed father. Geoff returned home late at night after a business trip just as a bad storm hit, with crashing thunder and flashes of lightning. When he got up to bed he found his two children, Alex and Carly, curled up in bed with his wife, Karen. Not wanting to wake the kids up, when it looked as though they had been too scared to sleep on their own, he slept in the spare room instead.

The following morning Geoff reassured the children that it was fine to get into bed with their mum when the weather was stormy and he was away, but that they should try not to when he was due back home.

After another work trip a few weeks later, Karen and the children turned up at the airport to welcome Geoff back. The plane was delayed so they parked and came in to wait in the arrivals hall, along with throngs of other people, for the plane's arrival. As Geoff came through the gate, his son Alex caught sight of him, and came running up shouting, 'Dad, Dad! I've got some good news!'

'What is the good news?' asked Geoff, giving him a hug.

Alex replied, still at top volume, 'The good news is that nobody slept with Mummy while you were away this time!'

The arrivals hall became oddly quiet, as everyone in the waiting area looked at the little boy, then at his father, and finally scanned the rest of the crowd to see if they could figure out exactly who his mummy was.

Mums are for food and dads are for playing and fun.
   Nicola — aged seven

Grandparents are a bit like tortoises, but they're human.
   Alex — aged four

Grandparents are very good at reading bedtime stories, so long as they don't fall asleep in the middle, which my grandpa sometimes does.
   Gail — aged nine

Father: And what will you do when you grow up to be as big as me?

Son: Diet.

A STAIRLIFT TO HEAVEN

One day, when Mrs Leyton was taking her grandchildren, Arthur, six, and Bella, four, to school they asked her, 'Granny, how old is Granddad?'

'Fifty-nine,' Mrs Leyton replied.

'And, Granny how old are you?' the two children asked.

'Fifty-eight,' she replied.

After a long pause, Arthur piped up, 'Are you and Granddad getting ready to go to heaven then?'

HOME SCHOOLING

Having taught his grandson, Andrew, to count up to ten, one grandfather thought it would be fun to teach him all the colours too, so he began pointing at objects and asking his grandson what colours they were.

'That post box over there, what colour is it?' he'd ask and Andrew would answer red. He got all the colours correct but then, when they had finished, Andrew turned to his grandfather and said, 'Grandpa, I really think it's time you should learn these yourself.'

Grandparents usually live at the airport or the train station. When we want them to visit we go and pick them up from there and when we've done with them visiting we take them back.

Tiffany — aged seven

WHERE'S MUM?

One day, two little boys noticed that their mum was lying asleep on the sofa in the living room. Wanting to know if she was just pretending or she really was asleep the boys giggled and whispered as they tiptoed all the way up to the sofa. Finally, the boldest of the two boys rushed up to the sofa, seized an eyelid, prised it open and leant forward to stare at the eyeball before rushing back to his brother.

'The good news is,' he told his brother breathlessly, 'Mum's still in there!'

PARENTING TESTS

A mother tells a story of when she was out for a walk with her four-year-old daughter, Ellen. While they were walking along Ellen picked up something from the ground and was about to put it into her mouth when her mother noticed and told her to put it back. The usual four-year-old response came back, 'But why, Mummy?'

'Well, Ellen, that's because it's dirty – it's been lying round on the dirty ground and probably has lots of nasty germs on it.'

Ellen looked up at her mum, eyes full of wonder, 'Mummy, how do you know so much about everything?'

Put on the spot, Mummy did a bit of ad-libbing, as all good parents do from time to time. 'Well, all mummys have to know this stuff. It's on the Mummy Test. You have to pass the test, otherwise they don't let you be a mummy.'

There were a few moments of silence as Ellen digested this new piece of information, before she piped up, 'So if you don't pass the test, do you have to be the daddy?'

'Exactly,' Mummy replied with a big smile on her face and joy in her heart.

Question to Lori, aged eight: What do your mum and dad have in common?

Lori: Both of them don't want any more kids.

BABY BLUES

When Samuel's mother gave birth to a new baby boy she and her husband decided it was time to move to a larger house. Listening in on the discussions Samuel interrupted his mum and dad.

'It's no use,' he said, 'he'll follow us wherever we go.'

Eric, aged six: Grandma, were you on board the Ark?'

Grandma: No, I was NOT on board the Ark!

Eric: Well, why weren't you drowned then?'

Question to Frankie, aged eight: How many brothers and sisters do you have?

Frankie: None. I'm a lonely child.

FUNNY KIND OF HOLIDAY

Two boys, aged six and eight, were in the car with their mum on the way to school. Their mum, looking at the late autumn clouds and thinking of the forthcoming visit from her mother, said to her two boys, 'Look at the clouds, boys, winter is coming. Do you know what that means?'

They both replied ecstatically, 'Halloween!'

Their mum said, 'Yes . . . and Grandma and Thanksgiving and Christmas.'

After a moment's silence her youngest son asked, 'Grandma's a holiday?'

> If it's your mother, you can kiss her anytime. But if it's a new person you have to ask for permission.
>   Roger — aged six

HERE COMES THE BRIDE

In Camilla Parker's family, her mother is known for being extremely emotional, particularly at weddings, when she would normally start sobbing the moment she spotted the bride. On one particular occasion, Camilla and her little sister Marjorie went with their mother to a cousin's wedding. They were all seated in the church and everything had fallen silent when Marjorie piped up (in a very loud voice), 'Mummy, Mummy, is it time to start crying yet?'

UP AGAINST A WALL

One young contestant on Michael Barrymore's programme *Kids Say the Funniest Things* had no compunction telling tales on his poor granny. When asked about a recent trip abroad he replied, 'We went to the Wailing Wall in Israel. The men were standing there, praying. My nan said, "Isn't it disgusting? It's terrible that!" She thought they were having a wee on the wall.'

REVISION

Two boys, Adam and Charlie, were upstairs in Charlie's bedroom revising for exams. Charlie says to Adam, 'We've got to be quiet. Granny's downstairs reading the Bible.'

'Oh,' replies Adam. 'Studying for her finals, eh?'

Andrew: Granny, hurry up and finish your dinner, please?

Granny: Why, Andrew?

Andrew: Because Dad says I can have a new train set when you've had your chips.

BABY NOISES

Daniel, aged five and a half, had had a very tough time getting used his new baby sister, Peggy, being in the family home. One day, as he was coming out of his bedroom talking very loudly, he was told by his mother to be quiet because his baby sister was fast asleep.

A couple of hours later when Peggy woke up and was screaming at the top of her lungs, Daniel walked up to his mother and said, in a very serious voice, 'Please tell Peggy to be quiet, my arm's asleep.'

TO THE RESCUE . . . OR NOT

As a young girl, Enid was training for her First Aid Certificate and over the course of the exam was asked the following question: 'What would you do if your little brother swallowed the key to your front door?'

Enid replied with unerring logic and great initiative: 'Climb in through the window.'

RELATIVE VALUES

Jeremy and his wife had long had plans to finally go and visit family in Oklahoma over the holidays and let their children get to know their American relations. Over the course of the journey, Jeremy and his wife talked about the trip and all the things they would see and people they would meet. When they were on the last leg of the journey, having listened patiently, their four-year-old asked, 'Who is our Uncle Homa, anyway?'

My mum's arms are nice and soft, like jelly.
    Suzie — aged four

MUMMY'S BOY

A little boy, when he was three, asked his father to buy him something in a shop. His father put him off saying, 'Sorry, son, we don't have enough money for that just now.'

His observant three-year-old son then piped up, 'Is that because Mummy holds the purse strings and she doesn't let you?'

Question to Rachel, aged seven: Do you ever help your mother clean the house, Rachel?

Rachel: No.

Question: What? Never?

Rachel: No, but I often help make the mess.

THE CITRUS FAMILY

Barbara was slicing grapefruit halves for breakfast when her daughter suggested they should have another baby in the family. Barbara, a bit taken aback, told her daughter that she thought a family of five was probably already quite large enough and asked why she wanted another sibling.

'Well,' her daughter reasoned, 'then the grapefruit would come out even.'

YOUNG LADY!

Three-year-old Eva waltzed up to her grandma in the kitchen one day saying, 'Old lady, will you help me wash my hands?' Eva's mother, shocked at her rude behaviour, asked why she had called her grandma that, and Eva replied, 'Well, she's allowed to call me "young lady".'

TOUGH CHOICES

When Steve and Sandra moved house they decided to drive both of their cars in convoy to their new home. Their eight-year-old son Nathan was extremely anxious about the journey and asked his father whether they might get separated. Steve replied soothingly that both cars would drive slowly, one behind the other, but Nathan still wasn't convinced.

'But what happens if other cars get between us and we lose each other?'

Steve replied, 'Well, in that case, I suppose we might never see one another again.'

'OK,' Nathan said. 'In that case I'm going in Mum's car.'

I think grandparents are amazing! Sometimes I wonder how mine are still alive.
    Charlotte — aged ten

MODELS OF EXTINCTION

A father recounts in *Babes and Sucklings* how he overheard his two sons, Mark, aged seven and Dominic, five, showing off their model dinosaurs to a child visiting the family home. Mark explained to the young visitor, 'That's a Stegosaurus, that's a Brontosaurus and that's a Tyrannosaurus rex.'

Feeling they were selling short the whole collection, the younger son chipped in: 'And we've got a granny upstairs.'

My grandma and God are very alike. They're both extremely old.
    Dora — aged six

LIGHTENING STRIKES

During a very long and violent thunderstorm on a hot summer's evening a mother was putting her little boy to bed. She was just about to turn the lights out in her son's room, when he had a last-minute panic and asked if she could stay and sleep with him.

'Sweetheart, you'll just have to be brave,' replied his mother, knowing this might be coming. 'I have to sleep in Daddy's room.'

Her son agreed, but then after a pause the mother overheard her son whisper, 'The big sissy.'

ODDS TO WIN

Many years ago, Mrs Cook's son wheeled his toy donkey up to her, when she noticed, lined up along the donkey's back, a whole row of coins.

Bemused, Mrs Cook asked her son why he had lined up the coins. Her innocent son replied, 'I'm putting money on a horse, like Daddy.'

My mother is very religious. She goes to play bingo at church every week, even if she has a cold.
    Annette — aged nine

CAUGHT NAPPING

An eighty-two-year-old grandfather recalls in *Little Gems* how he was having a leisurely afternoon nap on the sofa one afternoon when his granddaughter burst in the room with a young friend.

'Wake up, Granddad,' she demanded, jolting her grandfather out of his sleep. 'This is my new friend, Michael. He hasn't got a granddad and I've brought him in to show him what one looks like.'

CRACKING HEADS

This bizarre insight into parental relations is taken from Michael Barrymore's *Kids Say the Funniest Things*:

Barrymore: Do Mummy and Daddy ever fall out at home?

Daniel: Yes, a lot.

Barrymore: What do they fall out about, Daniel?

Daniel: My dad cracking an egg on my mum's head!

Question to Amy, aged three: Do you have a grandpa?

Amy (after some thought): Oh, yes, we've got one of those at Granny's house.

NEVER TOO OLD TO SHARE

One little girl was overheard talking to another in the children's section of a bookshop.

'Yes,' said the first girl, 'we've moved into a proper house now, so me and my brother have got a bedroom each.' Then, after a moment's pause, she added, 'But Mummy and Daddy still have to share.'

Grandma is brilliant at playing board games, but sometimes she falls asleep.
  Melissa — aged ten

My mum waxes my auntie's arms when she's got loads of hair on them.
  Jordan — aged seven

COMMON SENSE

Young Adam runs up to his father one day and says, 'Dad! Dad, I want to get married.'

His father looks surprised but says, 'OK, but really you need to have a girlfriend in order to do that.'

'But I've found a girl,' replies Adam excitedly.

'Who? What's her name?' asks Adam's dad.

'Grandma.'

'Wait a minute, let me get this absolutely straight. You want to marry my mother. You can't do that.'

'Why can't I?' says Adam indignantly. 'You married mine.'

JESUS LOVES THE LITTLE CHILDREN

Kids have their own unique and very funny ways of reasoning round the big theological questions of life: is there anyone up there? What does God look like? What are the words to the Lord's Prayer? The Lord does move in mysterious ways, so who's to say he doesn't look a bit like Grandma, or indeed live in a big coconut in heaven?

HAPPY BIRTHDAY!

A mother took her three-year-old girl to her first church service, which began with the lights being turned down and the choir members walking up the aisle in procession, carrying lit candles. All of a sudden the reverential silence was broken as the little girl started to sing loudly: 'Happy birthday to you, happy birthday to you…'

Our Father, who art in heaven, hullo, what is your name?
Five-year-old girl, overheard in a church in Taunton

Question to Yossi, aged six: What does God do?

Yossi: He's very good at making things. So is my mum. She bakes great cakes. I don't know if God makes cakes but he makes giraffes and things like that.

FIRST AND LAST

One contribution to *Little Gems* recounts how a young Sunday school vicar once asked his young wards what it was that Jesus did first thing in the morning and last thing at night, a practice that everyone should try to follow. Hoping for the correct answer (say his prayers), instead a lone little voice piped up from the back, 'Go to the toilet.'

HOW RICH WAS JESUS?

A young mother and her very inquisitive ten-year-old son were standing in an art gallery looking at a painting of the Nativity by Leonardo da Vinci.

'But I don't understand,' said the boy. 'Why wasn't he born in a proper bed with sheets and stuff instead of a manger? Because his father was God, wasn't he, so why couldn't he sort out something better than a shed?'

His mother patiently explained that Jesus's parents, Mary and Joseph, had been on a long journey at a very busy time of year and that even though they had tried to get a room at lots of inns in Bethlehem, there had been none left. 'Besides,' she added, 'they were very, very poor.'

'Well, they can't have been that poor,' replied her son, 'after all they did get a portrait done by Leonardo da Vinci.'

I know that God loves everybody, but he never met my sister.
Arnold — aged four

WHAT WOULD JESUS DO?

One Sunday after a church service, Tamsin asked her children what they had learned from the minister. Her daughter, who was in primary school and very bright, said, 'We learned all about Jesus and what he did.'

Tamsin was pleased that she'd remembered and asked her, 'And what did Jesus do?'

Quick as a flash her daughter replied, 'I don't know, Mummy, he wasn't there.'

HIDDEN MESSAGES

Lindsay was taking a reading session at a local school one day with Samba, aged seven, when they came across a new word in the book they were reading together – 'camouflage'. Lindsay proceeded to explain what the word meant: 'It's when something is hidden. So it's there, but you can't see it.'

After a long pause for reflection, Samba piped up, 'So, is God in camouflage then?'

HEAVEN'S ABOVE

A little boy, having already said his prayers asking for God to look after his mummy and daddy as well as all his various other friends and relations, then added: 'And please, God, look after yourself because without you we would all be in trouble.'

Question to schoolchild, Woking: What does God look like?

Schoolchild: God looks like a very kind ghost.

A MOTHER'S LOT

A Miss Rawley was teaching Sunday school one day and was describing how Lot's wife looked back over her shoulder as she fled Sodom, against the warnings of the angels, and was turned into a pillar of salt.

A little girl called Jane interrupted, 'My mummy looked back over her shoulder once when she was driving, and she turned into a telephone pole.'

Dear God,
I have read most of the Bible. I think you must be one
of the greats of writing of all time. My teacher thinks
Shakespeare is the best. She is wrong. He never did
nothing like floods and bushes and striking people dead
and bringing them back to life. He was like a text book in
school.
    You wrote a lot. Did you get anybody to type for you?
I am learning to type.
    Ray — aged eleven

WHISTLE A TUNE

During the vicar's prayer one Sunday morning, six-year-old Harry, who was sitting near the back of the church with his mother, let out a very loud whistle. Horrified, Harry's mother told her son to be quiet. After church she turned to Harry and asked, 'What on earth made you whistle in the middle of the vicar's sermon?'

Harry looked up innocently at his mother. 'I've been praying to God to teach me to whistle,' he replied, 'and just then he did!'

Question to schoolchild, Woking: Where does God live?

Schoolchild: He lives in a really big coconut in heaven.

GOD'S ONLY MISTAKES

A little girl, Frances, was watching her father, a vicar, who was sitting in his study one evening writing a sermon.

'Daddy,' she asked, 'how do you know what to say?'

'God tells me,' replied her father.

Frances paused, then said, 'So why do you keep crossing things out?'

Question to schoolchild, Woking: What does God look like?

Schoolchild: He might be thin air.

Dear God,
We have lots of fun down here on the land. You should visit us more. We even have a home for the old people so you would feel right at home. But they are not rich homes like you must have in heaven.
Maybe you would not like it that much.
     Will — aged eleven

A NEW HOME

After the long and very boring christening of his baby brother in church, David cried all the way home in the back seat of the car. His mother kept asking him what was wrong.

Finally, David replied, 'That priest said he wanted us to be brought up in a Christian home, and I want to stay with you and Daddy.'

THE GOOD SAMARITAN

Miss Phelps, a Sunday school teacher, was once explaining to her junior class the story of the Good Samaritan, and how the man in the parable was set upon by thieves, badly beaten and robbed. Miss Phelps described the man's injuries in detail so that her pupils got a good sense of how cruel the priest and the Levite were to ignore him, and of the compassion of the Samaritan who stopped to help.

Finally, she asked her class, 'So, if you saw a man lying on the side of the road wounded and bleeding, what would you do?

After an awed silence, one little girl at the back offered, 'I think I'd throw up, Miss.'

Our Father, chart in heaven. Hello, how be you then?
Overheard in a Somerset church

SERVICE ENDS

One little girl regularly went to a Catholic church where the service always ends with the priest saying, 'Peace be with you.'

'Mum,' she whispered impatiently one Sunday. 'Is it almost time to say, "Pleased to meet you"?'

SUNDAY BEST

During the Easter service at church all the little children in the congregation were invited to go up to the altar to meet the vicar. One little girl, Sandra, was wearing a pink and white dress with lots of flounces and ribbons.

The vicar leaned over and said, 'Oh my dear, what a pretty dress you're wearing. Is it your Easter dress?'

To which Sandra replied, loudly enough for the whole congregation to hear, 'Yes, but Mummy says it's a pain in the arse to iron.'

Our Father, who art in heaven, Halloween be thy name . . .

Jason — aged five

SSSHH!

Seven-year-old Rebecca and her little brother Stephen, aged four, were sitting in church together one day. Stephen was talking and giggling to himself – something which his older sister found extremely irritating. Just before their mother was about to intervene, Rebecca snapped.

'You're not allowed to be noisy in church,' she whispered crossly.

'Why not? And anyway, who's going to stop me?' replied Stephen.

Rebecca turned round and pointed towards the back of the rows of pews. 'Oh yeah? Can you see those two grown-ups by the door? They're hushers.'

Dear God,
You don't have to worry about me. I always look both ways.

Euan — aged six

PASS THE COLLECTION

A little boy was taken to church by his mother but soon became bored by the minister's sermon, which was dragging on and on.

'Mummy?' whispered the little boy leaning in towards her. 'If I give him the money now, will he let us go?'

WHAT DOES GOD LOOK LIKE

A mother tells this charming anecdote about her young son in *Little Gems*. He was then in primary school and very keen on drawing. His teacher enquired about one special-looking picture he had drawn.

'Who's this?' she enquired.

'It's a picture of God,' he replied.

His teacher smiled and said, 'But no one knows what God looks like.'

'Well, they will when they see this,' he replied.

Our Father, white shirts in heaven, Harold be thy name . . .

    Gerald — aged six

PRACTICE MAKES PERFECT

Four-year-old Caroline was once sitting on her grandmother's knee as she read her a fairy story. From time to time, Caroline took her eyes off the book and reached up to touch her grandmother's wrinkled cheek. She alternately stroked her own cheek, then her grandmother's.

Finally Caroline asked, 'Grandma, did God make you?'

'Yes, darling,' her grandmother answered. 'Of course, God made me a very long time ago.'

'Oh,' Caroline paused, then asked, 'Grandma, did God make me too?'

'Why, yes, indeed he did,' she replied. 'God made you just a little while ago.'

Feeling their respective faces again, Caroline observed, 'God's getting better at it, isn't he?'

WALKING ON WATER

A father tells the story of how his son had attended his first Sunday school class one summer's day. After he picked up his son and took him home he filled up their big paddling pool with water for his son to play in for the rest of the afternoon. After a while the father noticed his son scooping up the water in the paddling pool with his hands and throwing it on the grass.

'What are you doing?' he asked his son.

'Daddy, this water is broken so I'm getting rid of it!' came the reply.

'How do you mean it's broken?'

'Jesus could walk on top of his water, I just sink in mine.'

UNDERAGE

Zoe Watt's daughter, Phoebe, was five years old when she first went to a church service. She was fascinated by the ushers passing the plate round the congregation, watching everyone placing their money on it but when the ushers neared their pew she leant over and whispered (quite loudly): 'Don't pay for me Mummy, I'm under six.'

Question to Annie, aged seven: What does God look like?

Annie: He has long white hair and a long white beard and he's a bit smelly because he's very old and doesn't wash himself much.

THOU SHALT NOT

One day in school Miss Amersley was discussing the Ten Commandments with her class of ten-year-olds. After explaining in detail the commandment to 'honour thy father and thy mother', she asked if there was a commandment that teaches us how we should treat our siblings.

One little girl put up her hand and shouted out, 'Thou shalt not kill.'

God is up in Heaven looking after people. God is walking backwards and forwards thinking about fish.
James — aged six

WHO'D ADAM AND EVE IT?

A little boy called Jack came across the old family Bible one day. He began looking through it, fascinated by the old-fashioned pictures and yellowed pages. Something fell out onto the floor as he turned a page and he looked down to see it was a large leaf that has been pressed between the pages.

'Mummy! Mummy! Look what I found,' Jack called out.

'What have you got there?' asked his mother.

Eyes wide with wonder, Jack whispered, 'I think it's Adam's suit.'

Question to Amy, aged four: Why is it we should be quiet in Church?

Amy: Because people are sleeping?

FAVOURITE STORIES

Sarah College, a primary school teacher in the south-west of England, decided to do some Bible study with her pupils one day. She started by asking her class what their favourite Bible stories were. One little girl eagerly raised her hand.

'Please, Miss,' she said, 'my favourite story from the Bible is "Puss in Boots". It's really brilliant.'

Question to Carolyn, aged seven: What does God do?

Carolyn: He often does the cooking for Jesus. Jesus likes eating fish, I think he used to be a fisherman. I hate fish because they have too many bones.

QUIET PLEASE

The following story, which appeared in *Catholic School Kids Say The Funniest Things*, illustrates beautifully how catastrophically wrong things can go when a simple task is put into the hands of babes. During a rather long and tedious school Mass, a boy in one of the front pews started to talk to the child next to him. Not wanting to disrupt the service by getting up herself, one of the sisters asked the nearest child to quietly go up and tell him to stop talking. Misunderstanding her, the child went all the way up to the priest himself, interrupting him to say, 'Sister said you should stop talking.'

Question to Aaron, aged eight: What does God look like?

Aaron: Does he look like the Prime Minister but in nicer clothes?

ANIMAL LOVE

A Sunday school teacher was showing her class a picture of the Christian martyrs in a den of lions. One little girl looked so full of sadness and compassion as she studied the picture. Finally she exclaimed: 'Look at that poor lion right at the back. He isn't going to get any at all!'

DEDICATED SERVICES

Carl was five years old when his father took him to his first church service. They were slightly early so Carl's father pointed out a memorial plaque dedicated to all the men and women who had died during the First and Second World Wars.

'But what is it?' said Carl not really understanding its significance.

'It's our way of remembering all the people who died in service,' replied his father.

Carl stared at the plaque, full of concern, then looked up at his father. 'Which one? The morning service or the evening service?'

GOD SPEEDE

A little boy was running as fast as he could to church one Sunday morning.

'Please, God, don't let me be late!' he panted as he ran faster and faster. 'Please, God, don't let me be late!'

Suddenly he tripped over a broken piece of pavement and fell down, bruising himself and ripping his trousers. Getting up and brushing himself off, he set off again.

'Please, God, don't let me be late, but don't shove me either,' he added.

Dear God
If you let the dinasor not exstinct we would not have
a country. You did the right thing.
Jonathan — aged five and a half

DON'T BE RIDICULOUS

One day Reverend John Cartwright asked a young boy what his favourite story from the Bible was.

'I think it would have to be the one where Noah builds an ark and everyone sets sail for forty days and forty nights,' the boy said.

'Yes,' agreed the Reverend, 'that's a very good story and with all that water around them I bet they did a lot of fishing during the flood.'

The boy looked at him in astonishment. 'I don't think so,' he replied. 'After all, they only had two worms.'

Question to schoolchild, Woking: What does God look like?

Schoolchild: God doesn't look like anything much. He's a spirit.

SUNDAY SCHOOL

Miss Madison, a Sunday school teacher, once asked her class, 'Does anyone here know what the term "sins of omission" means?'

One little boy put up his hand. 'Please Miss,' he said, 'Aren't those the sins we should have committed, but didn't get round to?'

BED TIME

A priest was speaking to one of his parishioner's little boys, 'So, Charlie, your mummy says your prayers for you every evening, does she? That's very good, and what prayer does she say?'

Charlie looked up at the priest, all innocence. 'Well, she usually says, "Thank God he's in bed."'

ARE YOU STILL IN THERE?

A young boy, on hearing at his local church that God was everywhere, asked his mother, 'So, is God in the loo then?'

'Of course he is, darling,' replied his somewhat puzzled mother. 'Why did you ask that?'

'Because I just heard Daddy say, when the toilet door was locked, "Good God, are you still in there?"'

FRIENDS IN HIGH PLACES

Having gone to church one Sunday morning a mother and daughter were kneeling saying their prayers when the little girl began to giggle uncontrollably.

'Alice, be quiet,' the mother whispered.

'It's OK, Mummy,' Alice whispered back, 'I've just told God a really good joke and we are both laughing.'

Question to Grant, aged five: What does God look like?

Grant: I think he looks like my dad but a bit cleaner.

WHERE'S JESUS?

A young boy was visiting the school chapel with his parents on a tour of a Catholic school. The boy pointed to a model of the tabernacle and asked, 'What's in there, Mummy?'

The mother whispered to her son, 'Jesus is in there.'

After waiting by the tabernacle for a while, as his mother read an inscription, the boy finally asked, 'When's he coming out then?'

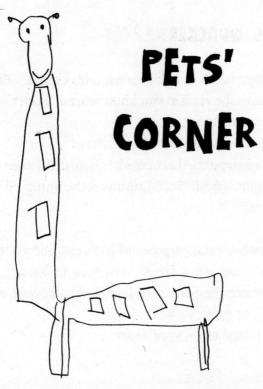

PETS' CORNER

Never work with animals or children, or so the old adage goes. And yet the resulting mayhem can be hugely entertaining for those fortunate enough to be looking on. There's no denying animals and children have a special bond; a pet can be as much a part of the family as a brother or sister (let's face it, usually more so) and zoos and wildlife hold their own magnetic allure for small minds, even if they occasionally get their natural history facts muddled...

ANIMAL QUACKERS

Toby's puppy fell ill one day, so his mother said, 'We must take Bertie to the vet. Do you know what a vet is?'

'No,' replied Toby.

'A vet is an animal doctor.'

Toby looked puzzled as he took this in, then, to get things quite straight, asked, 'So, Mummy, is the animal doctor a dog or a cat?'

Some fish are dangerous. Jellyfish can sting. Electric eels can give you a shock. They have to live in caves under the sea where I think they have to plug themselves into chargers.

Christopher — aged seven

ZOOLOGICAL

Harriet Steinberg, a primary school teacher, was walking around her class during a reading session one day when one of her usually well-spoken pupils pointed at a picture in a book about a zoo and said, 'Look at this! It's a frickin' elephant!'

Harriet took a deep breath. 'What did you call it?'

'It's a frickin' elephant! It says so on the picture.'

And so it did: African Elephant.

I think God made a mistake. I prayed for a puppy but
I got a baby brother instead.
   Rosie — aged six

I wish I was a dog so that Mum would tickle my
tummy more.
   Gerald — aged nine

THE AFTER LIFE

Cynthia Felstead overheard a conversation between her ten-year-old son, James, and her much younger daughter, Amy, who had just screamed on discovering a spider on the floor.

James stamped on the poor creature with his shoe. 'There you go Amy, I've killed it for you. It's dead. It can't hurt you any more.'

'Thank you,' replied Amy gratefully.

'Unless, of course, it comes back as a ghost in which case it will probably haunt you.'

I love my dog, Tinker. He's my pal, he is.
   Jonathan — aged three

FISHY BUSINESS

Being the pet of a small child is sometimes perilous. This extract from Michael Barrymore's *Kids Say the Funniest Things* shows how kids can love them, and then simply bin them.

Barrymore: Have you got any pets, Tyrone?

Tyrone: I had five fish.

Barrymore: You had five fish? And what happened to them?

Tyrone: They all died. The first one what died was black and kept on squeezing to the top and being greedy.

Barrymore: Did you bury the fish?

Tyrone: No – just chucked them out.

MAN OR DOG?

A man and his five-year-old son, Rick, were driving along the motorway when they passed signs for a racetrack. Rick saw the picture of the greyhounds and asked what happened there.

His father replied, 'It's where people go to race dogs.'

After a long pause, Rick said, 'I bet the dogs win.'

Did God mean for the giraffe to look like that or was it an accident?
   Norma — aged seven

BAD DOG

At the end of the day a policeman parked his van in front of the station. As he gathered up his equipment, a police dog in the back of the van started to bark, waiting to be let out.

A schoolboy came up and asked, 'Is that a dog in your van?'

'Yes,' the policeman replied, busy packing up his gear. He turned around to find the boy still standing there with a puzzled expression on his face: 'What did he do?'

Dear God
Please send me a pony. I never asked for anything before, you can look it up.
   Bruce — aged seven

Are zebras black or white? It's very confusing.
   Theo — aged six

CAT 22

In school one day, a little boy called Joey put his hand up to tell his teacher how he had found a dead cat lying by the side of the road the previous evening.

'How did you know the cat was dead, Joey?' asked his teacher.

'Because I pissed in its ear and it didn't move.'

'You did what?' asked the teacher, appalled.

'I said "pssst" in its ear,' replied Joey.

I love cats. They are warm and furry and have lovely pink noses. Why don't cats bark?
    Molly — aged five

KEEPING A NEUTRAL FACE

A teacher recalls a little boy in her class who came in and announced that his family had bought a new dog.

'She's called Pudge and we've had her neutered.'

The teacher, thinking that she would need to explain what neutering meant to the rest of the class, opened her mouth to begin, but she needn't have worried: the little boy went on, 'It means she can't have puppies. We got Mummy neutered too last year.'

I really want to get a pet tarantula but Mum doesn't like the idea. She says she'll go and live with Granny if I get a tarantula so Dad says I can have one for Christmas.

Billy — aged eight

A LITTLE BIT SMELLY

For some unknown reason little girls have long had a love affair with ponies and all things horsey, as the following story amusingly illustrates. Mr Blythe could never properly fathom his young daughter, Milly's, obsession with horses. One day he'd had enough: 'For heaven's sake, Milly,' he bellowed. 'Enough is enough! I can hardly move in this house without tripping over riding boots or some piece of tack or other. You're always late for your dinner, never seem to wear anything but dirty jodhpurs and all you ever babble on about is horses! Your hair is a mess, and you've actually begun to smell like a horse too!'

'Oh Dad!' said Milly, smiling from ear to ear as she ran up to hug him. 'Do I really smell like a horse? That's the nicest thing you've ever said!'

Digging in the litter box is not very exciting. You always find the same thing.
Bryan — aged nine

BOOZING FOR BEGINNERS

A grandmother had taken her three-year-old granddaughter, Madelyn, out for breakfast while the family schnauzer, Whisky, waited in the car.

Madelyn was, and is, a very chatty little girl and kept up a stream of conversation with the waitress as she brought them their pancakes and syrup. When they had finished eating, the waitress asked Madelyn what she was going to do with Grandma on their day together and Madelyn – standing up in the booth of the café for all to hear – said, 'Well, we have Whisky in the car . . .'

Giraffes would make good firemen, wouldn't they? People could just slide down their necks.
Amber — aged nine

NOT IN FRONT OF THE DOG

Mrs Robinson has a four-year-old daughter named Bella and one day the family decided to adopt a friendly and good-natured male cocker spaniel. Bella was having a bath one evening when suddenly the dog pushed the door and came bounding in.

Bella started screaming at the top of her lungs, 'No Mummy, he cannot come in!'

'Sweetheart,' her mother reassured her. 'It's just the dog!'

'But, Mummy, he is a boy and I am naked!'

NATURAL HISTORY

These were the first lines of a schoolboy's essay titled 'The Frog', which appeared in the collection *Pass the Port Again*. Though obviously wrong, they have a poetic logic all to themselves.

'A curious bird the frog are.

When 'e leap 'e fly almost.

When 'e sit down 'e sit on what 'e ain't got 'ardly.'

FURRY RELATIONS

This extract from Art Linkletter's *Kids Say the Darndest Things* shows just how fast some baby sisters can develop:

Linkletter: Any brothers or sisters?

Kid: A sister.

Linkletter: How old?

Kid: Month old.

Linkletter: What does she do most of the time?

Kid: Plays on the back fence.

Linkletter: How can she do that?

Kid: She's a cat.

My fish is strange. When I stick my nose up to the glass, he tries to eat it.

Jessica — aged ten

All in the Print

A five-year-old little girl called Melanie went with her dad to a farm to see a litter of kittens. On returning home, Melanie informed her mother that there were three male kittens and four female kittens. 'How did you know that?' her mother asked.

'Dad picked them up and looked underneath,' Melanie replied. 'I think it's printed on their bottoms.'

Going to the Zoo

A mother recalls in *Little Gems* how she took her five-year old daughter to London Zoo. They were standing in a crowd watching the chimpanzees. A very obviously male chimpanzee was lying on his back lifting a baby chimp up and down.

Her daughter said, 'Oh, look at that mummy chimpanzee playing with her baby.'

Without thinking, her mother said, 'That's not a mummy, it's a daddy.'

Quick as a flash her daughter said, 'Oh, of course it's a daddy. It's just lying around doing nothing.'

Sharks are ugly and mean, and have big teeth, just like Hanna Wright. She's not my friend no more.
   Dee — aged six

Question to Shante, aged six: What is your favourite animal?

Shante: My favourite animal is a horse because they gallop a lot and I like their hooves when they run.

THE BIRDS AND THE BEES

The birds and the bees is a topic that ties most parents up in knots, so it's hardly surprising that children are forced to resort to their own theories about how babies are made, and what teenagers and parents may or may not get up to behind closed doors. One thing is beyond a doubt: it's weird and disgusting and something you should put off for as long as possible – at least until you're fifty.

MOTHER'S TUMMIES

Josie, like many other children before and since, once presented her grandmother with this timeless conundrum: 'Grandma?' she asked. 'I know that babies come out of mothers' tummies, but how do they get there in the first place?'

WHERE DID I COME FROM?

Alicia Morgan writes about the time she was shopping for clothes for her five-year-old son Ben. She happened to absent-mindedly read out loud a label that said 'Made in Taiwan'.

To the amusement of a nearby shop assistant, Ben asked loudly, 'Mummy, was I made in Taiwan too?'

Dear God
I know all about where babies come from. I think.
From inside mummies, and daddies put them there.
Where are they before that? Do you have them in
heaven? How do they get down here? Do you have
to take care of them first. Please answer all my
questions. I always think of you.
      Yours truly, Susan

THE ARTS OF SEDUCTION

Jill, a teacher in a primary school, overheard the following exchange between two young pupils while they were standing in the dinner queue. They were in the process of discussing another member of staff who was pregnant and wondering when she might produce a baby.

One pupil turned to the other and said airily, 'If Mrs Jones doesn't hurry up and have her baby soon she'll probably have to be seduced.'

ASK ME ANYTHING

The following comes from an anecdote told by Monica Fletcher and appeared in the collection *Babes and Sucklings*. It's a story that beautifully sums up the excruciating torment of parents attempting to explain the birds and the bees to their offspring and the somewhat surprising responses they get in return.

Monica was driving her daughter to boarding school for the very first time and suffering from pangs of guilt that, at the age of eleven, she still hadn't had 'the talk'. Having bottled the discussion the night before, and still crippled with embarrassment, Monica once more broached the subject with her daughter, who sat, pale-faced and rigid, without saying a word, as her mother explained the whole thing in detail. Finally, and with a growing sense of desperation as they neared the last leg of the journey to school, Monica asked if she had understood, and if there was anything she wanted to ask her, anything at all.

Her daughter finally spoke, 'There is one thing, Mummy. I simply can't begin to fathom the Holy Trinity.'

I've got three girlfriends — Chloe, Becca and Paignton. They are all coming to live in my house. Becca and Chloe are going to sleep with me and Paignton can sleep on the sofa.
Connor — aged four

NAIL-BITING ENDING

Alan was a good boy who gave his parents very little trouble except for one thing; he liked to bite his fingernails. After several attempts to deter Alan with all kinds of horrid punishments if he didn't stop his nasty habit, his mother decided that she would play on her son's worst fear – that he would get morbidly obese.

That evening she informed him that the one thing that would guarantee massive weight gain was biting one's fingernails – a warning Alan took so seriously that in a matter of days he had completely stopped doing it. And all was well until a few weeks later.

Alan and his mother were out shopping in the local supermarket, when the little boy noticed a heavily pregnant woman in one of the aisles. Alan couldn't take his eyes off her. He stared and stared, until finally the woman walked up to him.

'Are you all right?' she asked. 'Do you know me?'

Alan shook his head. 'No,' he whispered, 'I don't know you, but I know what you've been doing.'

DATING GAME

A woman was at the park with her six-year-old niece when a little boy, about the same age, walked up to her and said, 'Do you want to be my girlfriend?'

To which the niece replied, 'Uh, no, only if I wanted a baby or something, which I don't.'

Julie says that when a boy slaps you he wants to kiss you. That's true.
    Small girl overheard in the park

A BUN IN THE OVEN

When Jayne was six months' pregnant with her second child, her firstborn child, Alexia, who was then four years old, was sitting on the bed while Jayne was getting ready to get into the shower. Alexia said, 'Mummy, you are getting so fat!'

Jayne said, 'Yes, poppet, but remember, Mummy has a new baby growing in her tummy.'

'I know that,' Alexia replied. 'But what's growing in your bum?'

Our new baby is a girl because her bottom goes all the way round.
   Jenny — aged four

SEX EDUCATION

Miriam had decided to teach the elder of her two daughters, Susie, all about the birds and the bees. Having related the finer details of how babies are made and thinking she had done a rather wonderful job, she was dismayed to discover her daughter was anything but impressed.

'That's disgusting!' exclaimed Susie. 'Really, really horrible. And to think you must have done it twice!'

WHERE DID I COME FROM?

The following little anecdote is not quite 'out of the mouth of a babe' but it presents a neat sidestep to the age-old discussion of the birds and the bees. A guest at a party given by the French writer Euphrasie Aubernon related a story concerning his young son.

His son had once asked him, 'Father, when you and Mother went to Italy on your honeymoon, where was I?'

'And how did you answer him?' asked another guest at the party.

'I told him,' replied the first guest, 'that he went there with me but came back with his mother.'

Kissing is yucky. I once saw my sister and her boyfriend kissing and it sounded like when Granny eats soup.
   Keira — aged seven

BIRDS AND BEES

Lord Horner tells a charming anecdote in *Pass the Port* about two young children who were at a gallery, examining a painting of Adam and Eve in Paradise. They were talking quietly together, little realizing their whispers were being overheard.

The girl asked the boy, who was slightly older, 'Which one is Adam and which one is Eve?'

After a moment's reflection, the boy replied, 'Well, I'm not quite sure, but I think I could tell if they had their clothes on.'

Question to Martin, aged eight: How would the world be different if people didn't get married?

Martin: There would be a lot of babies to explain, wouldn't there?

RELATIONS

A young girl came home from school one day having had a sex-education lesson.

Not realizing the momentous significance of the day, the little girl's mother asked, as usual, 'And what exciting things did you learn at school today?'

'We had a lesson about sex.' A pause as her mother nervously braced herself for more. 'Mummy, do you and Daddy have sexual relations?'

'Yes, darling, Daddy and I do have sexual relations . . .'

'Well then why haven't I met any yet?'

WHY?

The word 'why' is probably the most popular word amongst children and can often lead to amusing results as in the following story told by a mother, who reported a conversation between her and her four-year-old daughter.

'Why does Nana's dog have boobies?' asked the daughter.

'It's for her puppies to feed from. They get their milk from there. Like you and Dan had your milk from me when you were little babies.'

Daughter pauses for thought.

Then giggles uncontrollably.

Pause.

More uncontrollable giggles.

Pause.

'I did stop having your milk, didn't I?'

When I grow up I'm really going to like kissing lots of boys. Kissing boys is great — you make babies when you kiss boys. Jermaine in our class is a boy I'd like to kiss him but he keeps running away.

Janey — aged ten

I like mermaids. They are beautiful, and I like their shiny tails. How do mermaids get pregnant?
Helen — aged six

THE FOOD OF LOVE

A principal took three clever little girls out to McDonald's as a reward for winning a school competition. While they enjoyed their burgers, they chatted about what foods they liked and what they ate at home. One of the pupils disloyally said that her dad was terrible at cooking and that they got a takeaway whenever it was his turn to cook.

The second little girl chipped in to announce that her dad was a brilliant cook. The principal asked, 'What does he make?'

The little girl, eyes round with innocence, replied, 'He makes asparagus, candles and white wine. Then he and Mummy get in the jacuzzi.'

GOT MILK?

One of Art Linkletter's interviewees in *Kids Say the Darndest Things* shows just how much children quietly absorb from adult conversation. Of course it has to resurface later in the most embarrassing possible circumstances . . .

Linkletter: Who does your baby sister look like?
Kid: My mother.
Linkletter: And your oldest sister?
Kid: My father.
Linkletter: And you?
Kid: The milkman.
Linkletter: How so?
Kid: That's what my mother is always telling the neighbours.

THE SEX THING

Katie, aged six, came up to her mother one day, bright as a button, and announced, 'Mummy, I've found out what the difference is between boys and girls.' Katie pointed downwards with a big cheeky smile while her mother, Alice, wondered how she was going to tackle the delicate conversation that would no doubt ensue.

'That's brilliant, Katie! What is it?'
'It's all down below, Mummy.'
'Really?'
Here it comes, thought Alice.
'Boys have bigger feet.'

KISS, KISS, YUCK, YUCK!

Grandparents were visiting the family home of two little girls, Jamie and Alexis. Alexis, six, was doing her utmost to show Granny and Grandpa that she was far more grown-up than her baby sister, who was only two. Headstands, cartwheels and various dance routines followed, culminating with a song, her pièce de résistance.

'Barbie and Ke-en sitting in a tree,

P-I-S-S-I-N-G.

First comes love,

Then comes marriage . . .'

Both grandparents exchanged glances and Granny said, 'What was the word that you spelled out just then, Alexis?'

Alexis replied, 'Pissing. I learned it at school.'

Alexis's mother intervened at this point, 'Oh, darling! No, the song's meant to say "kissing", K-I-S-S-I-N-G.'

'Eugh, Mummy! No, that can't be it at all!'

Question to Theodore, aged eight: Is it better to be single or married?

Theodore: I don't know which is better, but I'm never going to have sex with my wife. I don't want to be all grossed out.

BIRTHDAY WISHES

Maisie was busy writing out a long wish-list of all the presents she wanted for her forthcoming birthday. Her mother asked her what, above all else, she would really like.

'A baby brother,' came back the reply. 'Pleeeeease!'

'But, darling,' her mother said, trying her best to explain, 'the thing is, Daddy and I would like to give you a baby brother, of course we would, but there really isn't enough time before your birthday next weekend to make it happen.'

'Why not?' Maisie replied, undeterred. 'You can do what Daddy does when he needs something in a hurry at work.'

'What's that?' asked her mother, looking a bit worried.

'Put more men on the job.'

BEAUTY AND THE LITTLE GIRL

American film actress Betty Grable (also known as 'The Pin-Up Girl') was once visited by her five-year-old niece who asked her Aunt Betty if she could join her in the bath.

'Sure,' replied the starlet. 'Climb right in.'

A little while later Betty noticed her niece staring at her. 'Is anything wrong?' she asked.

'I'm just wondering,' said the little girl, 'why it is that I'm so plain and you're so fancy.'

HOW TO HAVE A BABY

A retired schoolteacher recalls a conversation she had with a group of her pupils before classes one day.

'Lucy, why were you absent from class yesterday?' the teacher asked.

'Well, Miss, my mummy was having a baby.'

'How wonderful!' replied the teacher. 'Was it a boy or a girl?'

'I've got a baby brother, Miss.'

'That's lovely, Lucy. Do you know I'd like to have a baby too one day.'

'That's easy,' replied Lucy. 'All you have to do is have a warm bath, put on a fresh nightie and moan a lot.'

'Ooh, Mummy, look — those doggies are hugging each other!'

Elsie — aged three

DEAR SANTA

Christmas, as every good child knows, is all about shiny wrapping paper and new toys. Oh, and there's this fat bearded man in a red suit who's important, too. And something about donkeys and mangers. But mainly it's all about shiny paper and toys. Lots of toys.

Deer Santa
I hav bin very good this yer. I would lick the following.
motorbyke
Power Rangers
sweets
chocolate
a couple of guns (fake becas dad wont let me hav reel ones) so I can play with Billy
compooter
iplayer
but no clothes
thanks, Michael
ps. Can I have som hand cream for mummy?
Michael — aged eight

STEALING THE SCENE

Karen Bishop recently attended her daughter's nativity play. Right in the middle of the scene with all the shepherds and kings gathered around the crib, a little boy who was sitting in the audience whispered (in a very loud voice), 'Mummy, can we go home now and watch the TV?'

Dear Santa Claus,
My name is Robert. I am six years old. I want a rifle, a pistol, a machine gun, bullets, a hand grenade, dynamit, and tear gas. I am planning a surprise for my big brother.
        Your friend, Robert

MARY, MARY

Sylvia Parker's daughter, aged two and a half, spent the whole of the Christmas holidays singing, 'I wish I was Mary Christmas!' (to the tune of 'We wish you a Merry Christmas').

Question to Zoe, aged six: What would you like Father Christmas to bring you for Christmas?

Zoe: A turkey. But no sprouts.

CAROLING

A dutiful parent took a group of children to sing Christmas carols one December night. One of the children was overheard asking another, 'Where's Carol?'

Dear Santa,
What type of fuel do you use for your sleigh or are your reindeers just hyper? Either way, I hope you won't miss our house.
   Matt — aged eleven

IT'S NOT ME, IT'S HER!

Milly, who was two years old, and her sister Amanda, ten, had been doing a lot of fighting during the year – a not unusual occurrence between two siblings – particularly when the elder of the two is very strong-willed and bossy.

'I'm sorry, Amanda,' said the girls' mother, 'but I'm just going to have to tell Santa Claus about your dreadful misbehaviour. Milly's only little and doesn't know any better, but you should be grown up enough not to get into arguments with her.'

As she spoke, she picked up the phone and began dialling. Amanda's eyes grew large as saucers, and larger still when her mother began speaking into the receiver: 'Mrs Claus?' (The person on the other end of the line was, in fact, the girls' Auntie Gilly.) 'Could you put Mr Claus on the line, please?' Both sisters then heard their mother explaining to Santa (Uncle George) just how naughty they had been over the course of the year.

'Amanda, Santa wants a word with you,' said her mother handing her the phone. Santa Claus, whose voice was very deep and gruff, then explained to Amanda how there wouldn't be any toys for her to open on Christmas morning, because children who fight with their brothers and sisters aren't allowed presents. 'I'll be keeping a careful eye on you both from now on and will be expecting you to behave like good little girls between now and Christmas.'

Amanda nodded at every one of Santa's admonishments and silently hung up the phone. After a short time her mother then asked Amanda what Santa had said to her.

'What did he ask, darling?' she said.

In a tiny little voice Amanda said very calmly, 'Mummy, he said he won't be bringing Milly any toys this year. Sorry.'

Question to Daniel, aged seven: What did the three wise men bring Jesus as gifts?

Daniel: I know for his birthday he got money and gold from the Wise Men but I would have given him a Liverpool kit.

THE LEAD ROLE

When Melinda's son, Stan, was seven years old, his school put on a nativity play and he was asked whether he'd like to be a sheep, a donkey, an ox or a mouse. His answer: 'I want to be a Tyrannosaurus rex.'

Dear Santa,
I got an A in maths. Will you please remember my A when you get to my stocking? I hope I didn't get the A for nothing.
   Lots of love Rebecca

NO ORDINARY CHRISTMAS

A few years ago Helen Markov and her husband took their little girl, Tish, to see Father Christmas in his grotto at their local garden centre. All was going well until Tish asked Father Christmas where he lived.

'Lapland,' he replied.

'Oh,' replied Tish. 'It's just that those sandwiches on the table there say Marks and Spencer. Did you buy them on your way over?'

Question to Jimmy, aged five: What is the meaning of Christmas?

Jimmy: Was it when Jesus was hung up on a cross and died and then God said he could live with him in Heaven?

CHRISTMAS CHEER

As Christmas approached one year, a father asked his little girl what she would like as her main present. Without hesitation, she said that what she really wanted was a baby sister to play with, which was lucky because her mother did indeed return from hospital on Christmas Eve having just given birth to a little girl.

When her father asked her the same question the following year, the little girl thought long and hard, before replying, 'If Mummy won't find it too uncomfortable, I'd like a Shetland pony.'

There were a lot of animals in the manger including donkeys, camels, cows and jellyfish.
    Ruth — aged eight

LAST ORDERS FROM LAPLAND

Robert Granger tells of a conversation he had with his young grandson, David. He had asked David whether he knew what he wanted from Father Christmas that year. David pulled out an extensive list.

When Robert expressed surprise on the sheer length of it, his grandson replied: 'Well, next year I might not believe in him.'

Dear God
Thanks for the bike last Christmas Day. It has made me very happy except for May 13 at 4 o'clock when I rode into a big ditch that I did not see.
I am okay.
    Spenser — aged ten

ALLELUIA!

Natalia was picked up by her dad from Sunday school just before Christmas, and on the way home he asked her what they had studied that day.

Natalia answered, 'Well, when Mary heard she was the mother of Jesus, she sang the Magna Carta.'

FESTIVE TOPPINGS

Three-year-old Charlie Peston drew back the curtains one December day after it had snowed all night. Looking at the white coating on everything, he looked up at his mum, overcome with excitement: 'Ooooh, cake, Mummy!'

Question to Jane, aged six: What kind of animals were in the manger when Jesus was born?

Jane: There was a donkey, a sheep and a cow there as well as Mary and Joseph. It sounds quite crowded.

MARY CELESTE

A teacher asked her class if they knew the name of Jesus's mother.

'Mary,' replied one little boy.

'Very good,' said the teacher. 'Now who can tell me the name of Jesus's father?'

'Please, Miss, it's Verge,' said a little girl.

'Verge?' replied the teacher somewhat puzzled.

'Yes,' said the little girl confidently. 'Verge an' Mary.'

EARLY CHRISTMAS

Several years ago now, Emily Jaynes's youngest daughter, Alison, rushed into their kitchen excitedly.

'Mummy! Mummy!' she shouted. 'You know I wanted a doll's house for Christmas?'

'Yes,' Emily said slowly, 'why are you asking?'

'Because I don't need it now. I just found one under your bed!'

Dear Santa Claus,
How many days do you have to be good? I have been good for two days and I will try again on Monday.
I love you. Christina

THREE WISE MEN AND A LEOPARD

Fiona Barker's daughter, Becca, once came home from school in a state of huge excitement after parts had been announced for that year's nativity play. Becca said she was going to play a leopard, which puzzled her mother somewhat, who then wondered whether perhaps the play was going to be themed on a film, like *The Jungle Book*. The next day, when Fiona dropped off her daughter at school she went up to speak to Becca's form teacher about the costume and to say how excited Becca was to be playing the part of a leopard. The form teacher looked astonished and then laughed. 'Amy isn't playing a leopard, Mrs Barker, she's playing a shepherd!'

The meaning of Christmas is igloos. You get to make really great igloos.
    Schoolchild, Woking

MR FROSTY

When Anita Cullen's son, Damon, was about three years old there was large fall of snow over Christmas, and one morning they went outside to build a snowman in the garden. They rolled two big balls of the stuff and gave 'Mr Frosty' a carrot for his nose, stones for his eyes, grass for his mouth, and then added an old hat and scarf to keep him warm.

When they had finished adding the final touches, Damon looked up at his mother and said, 'Mummy, you do realize he's not a real person, don't you? He's only made of snow.'

Question to schoolchild: What is the meaning of Christmas?

Schoolchild: Is it Rudolph?

CHRISTMAS LIES

Tim, a seven-year-old boy, was asked to say a thank-you prayer before the family dug in to their Christmas dinner. Everyone seated round the table bowed their heads and waited for him to speak.

'Dear Lord,' began Tim, 'thank you for Mummy and Daddy and my brother Euan and my sister Daisy and all my uncles and aunts and granny and grandpa. Thank you also for bringing us this yummy turkey and potatoes and carrots and leeks and stuffing and the cranberry sauce and the Christmas pudding . . . ' then there was a long pause before suddenly Tim whispered, 'If I thank God for the Brussels sprouts, he'll know that I'm lying, won't he?'

THE WORLD ACCORDING TO KIDS

It's tough being small – there's a big world out there and such a lot of information to take on board about how it works, who runs it and what exactly grown-ups are so busy doing all the time. In the world according to kids, the equator is an imaginary lion (which would make it so much more interesting), the Jews had problems with their genitals for many years and the Queen likes to eat fish fingers and peas and uses washing-up gloves to do the dishes afterwards, which, as everyone knows, is quite true.

Always Ask the Police

While making out a vandalism report at a primary school, the local police sergeant was interrupted in his duties by a little boy about six years old. Looking up and down and examining the police officer's uniform the boy asked, 'You're a policeman, aren't you?'

'Yes,' replied the officer, who then continued to write up his report.

'My mum says that if I ever need help I should always ask a policeman or -woman. Is that right?'

'Yes, lad,' came back the reply. 'That's right.'

'Well then,' the little boy asked, 'can you take me to the toilet, please?'

Three kinds of blood vessels are arteries, vanes and caterpillars.
    Schoolchild — aged ten

We do not raise silk worms in the United States, because we get our silk from rayon. He is a larger worm and gives more silk.
    Alvin — aged nine

BACH TO THE FUTURE

The following potted biography was handed in to one schoolteacher, who must have wondered how so many facts could get so muddled: 'Johann Bach wrote a great many musical compositions and has a large number of children. In between he practised on an old spinster which he kept up in his attic. Bach died from 1750 to the present.'

Beer must be a good thing. My dad says the more beer he drinks the prettier my mum gets.
    Tommy — aged six

THE PRIME MINISTER'S DAD

One father describes when his eight-year-old daughter was sitting with her parents while they watched the news one night. Prime Minister at the time, Gordon Brown, then appeared in an interview clip. The little girl suddenly piped up and said, 'Is that the Prime Minister? I prefer his dad, Gordon Bennett.'

If you are surrounded by sea you are an island. If you don't have sea all around you, you are incontinent.
    Wayne — aged ten

When boats had sails, they had to use the trade winds to cross the ocean. Sometimes, when the wind didn't blow the sailors would whistle to make the wind come. My brother said they would be better off eating beans.
William — aged nine

THE DIFFERENCE BETWEEN US

This wonderful story, which first appeared in *Pass the Port*, perfectly illustrates how children can unwittingly turn grown-up ideas on their head, in this instance the sectarian divide in Northern Ireland is reduced to a mere technicality, which it probably should be.

A little boy, who was the only child of parents who lived to the north of the Ulster–Eire border, was asked to go for a picnic with a little girl, who was the only child of parents on the south side of the border.

It was a sunny, hot July day and they picnicked by a river. The children took all their clothes off and played in the water.

When the little boy got home his mother said to him, 'Was it interesting?'

He replied, 'Yes, Mummy, it was fascinating. I never knew before what a big difference there is between Protestants and Catholics.'

MICHAEL WHO?

The following is an extract from one of Bill Cosby's interviews on the TV show *Kids Say the Darndest Things* that shows how not even the greatest artists in history are spared the cheek of children.

Cosby: Did you ever hear of an artist named Michelangelo?

Raymond: Michael who?

Cosby: Michelangelo. That was his whole first name.

Raymond: He had another one after that?

Cosby: Yes, and I really don't know why. At any rate, he was so inspired by the Bible that he painted the whole story of Creation on the ceiling of a chapel in Vatican City. You know where that is?

Raymond: In Canada?

Cosby: Close, in Rome.

Raymond: That's kinda crazy.

Cosby: That the Vatican City's not in Canada?

Raymond: No, I mean painting stuff on the ceiling. Why didn't he put it on the walls? You can see them better.

Cosby: Maybe he wasn't a genius after all.

Raymond: Well, I never heard of him.

The equator is an imaginary lion which runs around the middle of the earth.
Hannah — aged nine

OUT OF THE MOUTHS OF BABES

In the book *Little Gems*, one teacher recalls her post teaching in an inner-city infant school. Many of the children, although from poor and often difficult backgrounds, were warm and loving. The teacher was one day reading the story of 'The Three Little Pigs' to the assembled class and got to the part where the Big Bad Wolf was huffing and puffing to blow down the house of straw and gobble up the first little pig.

'The bastard!' came a small voice from the back.

ON ROYALTY

When Sarah Smith, aged six, was asked what she knew about the Queen, the comprehensive and illuminating reply came back, 'The Queen eats peas, fish fingers and mashed potatoes. She wears rubber gloves to wash up in the sink.' Perhaps she does.

If I were in charge of the world I would make it okay to spit in public because it is fun and I am good at it.
Jimmy — aged seven

There are twenty-six vitamins in all, but some of the letters are yet to be discovered. Finding them all means living forever.
Schoolchild — aged ten

Ancient Egypt was old. It was inhabited by gypsies and mummies who all wrote in hydraulics. They lived in the Sarah Dessert. The climate of the Sarah is such that all the inhabitants have to live elsewhere.
From a school essay

My Dad is always on the golf course. He doesn't like playing golf that much but he's hoping his boss is going to give him a pay rise.
Grant — aged eight

PEOPLE IN HIGH PLACES

When Jake, aged eight, was asked what he knew about the Queen for Michael Barrymore's *Kids Say the Funniest Things*, he painted a rather more spectacular and lavish lifestyle than Sarah Smith – although, bizarrely, peas still feature: 'The Queen of England lives in a huge palace with fountains, and slides for children. She has bacon, egg, sausages, beans on toast and orange juice for breakfast, and steak, turkey, peas, spaghetti, gravy, pud and cakes.'

Question to Lucy, aged seven: Who is the Prime Minister of Britain?

Answer: The Prime Minister is called David Cameron but I think his wife just calls him David.

When men went to fight in the wars their wives were left alone and that caused havoc because they tarted about, causing the population to rise.
    From a school essay

PRESIDENTIAL CORRESPONDENCE

The President of the United States gets, literally, tons of letters every year. The following missives illustrate the range of bizarre and probing questions the President receives daily, the first two are extracted from *Thanks and Have Fun Running the Country*, while Eliana's comes from the *Kids' Letters to President Obama*, both wonderful collections.

Dear President Obama,
Here is a list of the first ten things you should do as president:
1. Fly to the White House in a helicopter.
2. Walk in.
3. Wipe feet.
4. Walk to the Oval Office.
5. Sit down in a chair.
6. Put hand-sanitizer on hands.
7. Enjoy moment.
8. Get up.
9. Get in car.
10. Go to the dog pound.
    Chandler Browne (aged twelve)

Dear President Obama,

Are you going to be pictured on our money? How do you get in the White House? Do you like Abraham Lincoln? Do you have a big backyard? Martin Luther King Jr. had big fans. How many fans do you have? You could help us by giving us food. I am Luis Ramirez. I go to school at Mayberry. I like to play video games.

Luis Ramirez (aged eight)

Dear President Obama,

Can I come over for a sleepover with Sasha at the White House? I've never been to a sleepover before and that would be super fun!

Your friend,

Eliana (aged six)

Question to Alicia, aged eight: What does the Queen look like?

Alicia: Dad says she's like the back end of a bus . . . what does that mean?

Charles Darwin was a naturalist. He wrote the Organ of the Species. It was very long and people got upset about it and had trials to see if it was really true. He said God's days were not just 24 hours, but without watches who knew anyway?

From a school essay

If I ruled the world I would ban teachers from being bossy and I'd make all vegetables pink.

Gillian — aged six

Question to schoolchild, Woking: Who is the Prime Minister?

Schoolchild: Is he the one who just became the government? Oh, yeah — he's my mum's brother's friend.

Question to Aimee, aged six: What does the Queen look like?

Aimee: Mummy says she looks like Stanley Baxter but with really nice pearls.

TEACHERS BEWARE

A professor told a story in *Pass the Port Again* which perfectly illustrates the relentless logic in the way children view the world. A young teacher who had recently graduated from teacher training college took up her first post at a progressive local school.

On the first day she was proud of the rapport she had built up between herself and her pupils so, in the last half-hour of the school day, she decided to put into practice some of the more progressive methods of teaching she had studied at college – namely how to make pupils search for knowledge themselves.

'Now class,' she said, 'in the last couple of minutes I want to explore the world we live in.'

The children were really excited at the prospect of doing this; one of them, a boy called Johnnie, put up his hand, 'Please, Miss,' he said, 'What is the weight of the world?'

The teacher was suddenly at a loss how to answer. Despite having taken a Masters Degree in Geography and afterwards taking a Bachelor of Education degree, nothing had provided her with the answer to Johnnie's question. Finally, realizing she'd need to resort to the teacher's favourite get-out clause, she said, 'Johnnie, that's an excellent question. In fact it's so good I suggest you and your parents stop off at the library on the way home and look up the answer there.'

The bell rang for the end of class and everyone left

including the teacher, who subsequently rushed to the local library herself to find the answer.

The next day, the teacher began her lesson by saying: 'Well, class, who can tell me how much the world weighs?'

Nobody answered, so finally – feeling rather smug – the teacher said, 'Okay, it was a very difficult question but the answer is 5,887,613,230,000,000,000 tons.'

Still, none of the children said anything except little Johnnie who put up his hand again. 'Please, Miss,' he said, 'is that with or without people?'

The Jews were a very proud and noble people, but throughout history they had problems with Genitals.
    Robbie — aged ten

When I'm made Prime Minister I'd make my mum Mrs Prime Minister.
    Gavin — aged seven

If I were in charge of the world I would make it law that children could eat as many sweets as they wanted and when they were sick no one would say 'I told you so!'
    Nigel — aged eight

COMING OR GOING?

The following was one of TV and radio presenter Art Linkletter's favourite after-dinner stories because it always made people laugh and one can easily see why.

'Mum?' asked a small boy. 'Is it true that we're dust before we're born?'

'Why, yes,' replied his mother, 'I believe that is true.'

'And, Mum, is it also true that we're dust after we're dead?'

'Of course,' replied his mother in an increasingly puzzled tone. 'Why do you ask?'

'Well, come up to my bedroom and look under my bed, quickly please! Somebody's either coming or going!'

STOP PLAYING WITH YOUR FOOD

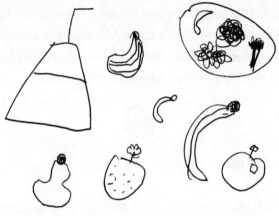

Pick a child at random and at the top of their list of special treats will usually be ice cream, chocolate and sweets – bottom, for some reason, is always sprouts (but then again, the same could be said of grown-ups, if they answered truthfully). Children have imaginative ideas about the stuff on their plates: do jelly beans really get made in squidgy factories? Why can't spinach taste like chocolate cake? If a jelly wobbles is it still alive? And no matter how often you tell them otherwise, they will always, always play with it.

THANDWICHES

This charming conversation was reported by Winifred Lewis in *Babes and Sucklings*. Her sister's two grandchildren were hosting a pretend tea party. Ann, aged six, and Sarah, four, had a baby sister who was still being breastfed. When the choice of what they would have to eat arose (both sisters having a lisp), Ann said, 'We'll give them Marmite thandwiches and some chocolate bithkits. But what can we give the baby 'cos she only eats boothums and we haven't got any?'

YUM YUM

At his birthday party, a little boy ate a huge amount of sausage rolls, cream buns and birthday cake. When his mother scolded him saying, 'Robbie, if you have another slice of cake, you'll go pop!', Robbie replied fearlessly, 'Well then, give me another slice of cake and stand back.'

Question to Kerry, aged five: Would you like some more coca cola, Kerry?

Kerry: No, thank you. It might give me a fizzy bottom.

TURN THE SOUND DOWN!

Three-year-old Lucy was sitting having her breakfast in the kitchen, while watching her favourite cartoon on the corner TV. Meanwhile her mother was frying sausages in a pan. The sizzling obviously started to intrude on Lucy's enjoyment of her cartoon so she turned round to her mum to say politely, 'Please turn the sound on the sausages down, I can't hear the TV.'

Does the Easter Bunny lay chocolate eggs?
    Astrid — aged four

YOU'RE SO CLEVER

One mum had cooked a special meal for her whole family to mark the start of the school holidays. Her six-year-old son, visibly impressed, said, 'This is a yummy dinner, Mummy!'

His mother replied, pleased at the compliment, 'Thank you, darling! I'm glad you like it.'

Then he asked, 'Did you cook it from scratch?'

His mother said that she had indeed.

To which her son replied, 'I didn't know you could cook like this all by yourself!'

HOW VERY TASTELESS!

Kids have an often suicidal disregard for food hygiene, as this story (and many more like it) amply demonstrates. Jenny was taking her eight-year-old son round the supermarket with her one day. He was eating a packet of sweets as they went up and down the aisles, but every so often he would accidentally drop one or two on the floor.

Jenny didn't notice until he dropped a whole handful and proceeded to pick them up off the floor and put them into his mouth. She intervened saying, 'That's disgusting. There's germs all over those!'

He looked up at her thoughtfully, 'Yes, but you can't really taste them.'

Question to schoolchild, Woking: Where do jelly beans come from?

Schoolchild: A squidgy factory.

GRACE

Six-year-old Annie and her parents were enjoying a Sunday roast at her grandmother's house. They were all in the dining room, seated around the table as Granny served up the lovely food. When Annie took her plate she tucked in straight away.

'Darling,' cried Annie's mother, 'you've got to wait until we say a prayer.'

'But I don't have to,' replied Annie.

'Of course you have to,' said her mother. 'We always say a prayer before eating.'

'That's in our house,' Annie explained, 'But this is Granny's house and Daddy says she knows how to cook.'

My favourite food is chocolate ice cream, and then Mummy's apple crumble. But they are better both together.
Russell — aged ten

DIZZY EGGS

At the age of five, Florence was helping her mother to bake an enormous chocolate cake. After the eggs were carefully cracked and poured into the bowl, she eyed the mixer and enquired, 'Can I make them dizzy now?'

ANIMAL OR HUMAN?

The following conversation was reported on BBC Radio 4's programme *Quote … Unquote*. Mary Shippey had overheard two small boys discussing their lunch.

The first boy, aged three, announced, 'We had custard for lunch today.'

The second boy, aged four, asked, 'Was it Bird's custard?'

To which the first replied, 'No, it was people's.'

JELLY, ANYONE?

When Susan Wall's daughter was about five years old she decided to make her a jelly for tea as a treat. Having made the jelly in her favourite flavour (strawberry) she put it on a huge plate and set it down before her daughter with a spoon so she could eat it. It wobbled beautifully but to Susan's surprise her daughter burst into tears.

'What's wrong?' Susan asked, feeling worried.

'Mummy,' she wailed. 'It's not dead yet!'

I DON'T FEEL TOO GOOD

Ali, aged four, was drinking some juice when she got a bad case of the hiccups. 'Please don't give me this orange juice again,' she said. 'It makes my teeth cough.'

Bubbles get into lemonade because the people in the factories all jump up and down with the bottles.
     Joshua — aged five

WHEN THE CHIPS ARE DOWN

A little girl called Jessica was chatting to her grandfather on the phone one spring day. Her grandfather asked if her mother had planted any vegetables in the back garden yet – and suggested they could grow potatoes so that later in the year they could use them to make chips. Jessica giggled uncontrollably as she said, 'Grandpa, don't be silly! You don't get chips from the ground, they come from McDonald's!'

DON'T EAT ALL THE SWEETS

Sylvia Llewelyn-Davies, mother to the children who inspired J. M. Barrie to write *Peter Pan*, once told a story about her young son to a group of her friends.

On seeing her son, Jack, tucking into a whole plate of confectionery, she told him, 'You'll be sick tomorrow if you eat any more chocolates.'

'No,' he replied cheekily, as he helped himself to another one, 'I'll be sick tonight!'

MOTHER'S MILK

Rosie Edwards recently asked her five-year-old son, Toby, where milk comes from – thinking he would answer 'a cow' – but instead he said, 'Tesco's!' with a large smile at how clever he was.

PANCAKE DAY

In the kitchen one day, a mother was cooking her two young sons, Kevin and Mark, pancakes for dinner when they began to argue over who was going to have the first one. Immediately their mother saw this as the perfect opportunity for a lesson in morals.

She said, 'Boys, if Jesus were here he would say, "Let my dear brother have the first pancake. I can wait."'

Quick as a flash Kevin turned to Mark and said: 'Okay, Mark, you be Jesus.'

The thing I like best is chocolate cake. Why can't they make vegetables and spinach and stuff like that taste like chocolate cake?
Rowenna — aged six

A CHILD'S EYE VIEW

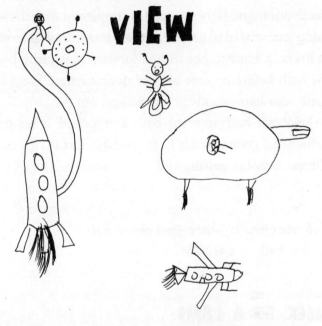

Sometimes kids can utter a one-liner that stops you in your tracks – such as when one little girl, noticing all the dancers at the ballet were on tiptoes, asked why they didn't just get taller dancers. Or another child who, when asked what sort of garden she would like, suggested a kindergarten. Well, it makes sense doesn't it? Children simply apply an innocent logic to the world that we adults, poor us, lost somewhere along the way.

BATHTIME

Maya Johnson was helping her six-year-old son, Jacob, take a bath one night. Jacob was getting impatient with the whole thing and started to get out of the water with shampoo still in his hair. His mother rushed forward to get him back in the bath before he shot out the door, saying, 'We need to rinse your hair quickly before you get out.'

Jacob sat back into the bath and looked at his fingers (which had gone wrinkly in the suds) before saying crossly, 'Oh no, now I'm getting old!'

A cemetery is where dead people live.
  Ruth — aged six

MEEK AS A LAMB

When he was a small boy, the English poet and celebrated essayist Charles Lamb was taken by his older sister, Mary, for a walk in their local cemetery. He was an astute little boy, even then, and began reading out the epitaphs on the headstones as they passed them, commenting on all the 'virtuous', 'beloved', 'charitable' people who were buried there.

'But Mary,' he asked at last, 'where are all the naughty people buried then?'

Mother: Amanda, are you telling me the truth?

Amanda: Yes I am.

Mother: Are you sure because you have a cheeky little grin all over your face?

Amanda (rubbing her cheeks): Where? Where do I have a grin?

CUT THE CANT!

American comedian Eddie Cantor recalled a day when, on leaving the theatre after a performance in Wichita, Kansas, he paused outside the stage door to sign autographs for a group of children who had been waiting for him to exit. Noticing a small boy who was standing to one side of the group Cantor asked him 'Don't you want my autograph too?'

'Hell, no,' replied the boy. 'I was waiting for you to get through with your act so I can see Donald Duck.'

A CLOSE SHAVE

One father, who had had a beard for many years, decided one day to shave it all off. He went up to his five-year-old daughter while she was busy playing to see what she would make of the new look.

'Do you notice anything different about me today?'

She looked puzzled, not yet able to spot what had changed. 'No.'

'My beard's gone.'

Comprehension dawned and then she said, 'Well, I didn't take it.'

DUCKING UNDER

According to Lord Oaksey on the BBC Radio 4 programme *Quote . . . Unquote,* the following exchange was overheard at a local swimming pool, where a little girl could be seen splashing water over a little boy.

'I'm going to duck you,' shouted the little girl.

'No, chance,' replied the young boy. 'You can't even say it proper.'

CHECKOUT CHARM

While queuing up at the checkout at the local supermarket, one woman's son took a shine to the lady at the till, and said, all charm, 'You have such lovely yellow teeth.'

HOME TRUTHS

The following exchange between a mother and a daughter has appeared in so many different collections of stories and anecdotes, it's obviously one that strikes a special chill in mothers' hearts.

One evening, a young mother was sitting at her dressing table applying some face cream, when her young daughter entered the bedroom and sat down beside her.

'Mummy, is that the cream they show on TV that makes you beautiful?' Her mother replied that it was, and thought fondly of how much fun she would have as her daughter grew older, trying out clothes and make-up together.

Meanwhile her daughter pondered for a moment before saying, 'It doesn't work very well, does it?'

TRUE COLOURS

A mother was attending a meeting with her daughter's schoolteacher one afternoon. The teacher held up a tan piece of card and asked the little girl, 'Do you know what this colour is?'

The little girl replied, 'No.'

The teacher then explained, 'This colour is tan.'

Then, to her mother's embarrassment, her daughter brightened and said, 'Oh yes, Mummy gets one of those out of a bottle!'

Mummy, it's raining dumplings!
Mary — aged three (on seeing hail)

DON'T BE SO STUPID, MUM!

A mother tells of teaching her three-year-old son his 'ABC's' one day.

'Apple starts with . . .?' she said.

He answered correctly, 'A'.

'Boy starts with . . .?'

Again, he answered correctly, 'B'.

So she asked him, 'What does car start with . . .?'

His reply was, 'DUH, Mummy, a key!'

AND WHO CREATED YOU?

The American humorist and creator of many well-loved children's books, Dr Theodore Seuss, once received a fan letter from an eight-year-old which said, 'Dear Dr Seuss, You sure thunk up a lot of funny books. You sure thunk up a million funny animals . . . who thunk you up, Dr Seuss?'

> Question to Mark, aged five: When will you turn six, Mark?
>
> Mark: When I'm tired of being five.

RETURN TO SENDER

A retired circuit judge told in *Pass the Port Again* of a case he had heard in a magistrate's court in the Midlands. A small boy was giving evidence against the defendant. The boy was deemed by the magistrates to be too young to understand the full meaning of 'swearing on oath' and so he was allowed to go ahead and give evidence, after being sternly told to answer as truthfully as he could.

The prosecuting solicitor began proceedings and was excessively cautious about asking leading questions – so as not to appear to be influencing the little boy's answers. He managed to get the boy to tell him his full name and his house number and street, but the lawyer was having great difficulty coaxing out the name of the boy's village. On his final attempt, he tried a new tack and asked him, 'If I wrote you a letter I would have to write down your name and "10 Broad Street" on the envelope, and what else would I have to put on it?'

'A stamp,' came the prompt reply.

DON'T LOOK UP!

J. M. Barrie, the playwright who wrote *Peter Pan*, told the following anecdote, concerning a young boy who had come to see the play and been given a seat in the author's private box. When he was asked, at the end of the production, what he thought of the play the little boy paused to think and then said: 'What I think I liked best was tearing up the programme and dropping the bits on people's heads.'

CAN YOU SMELL ANYTHING?

It was Sarah-Jane's birthday and her parents gave her a beautiful wrist watch and a bottle of sweet-smelling perfume. She was delighted and spent all day showing off her gifts to everyone she came across. Finally, it started to get tedious for the rest of the family and her party guests and her mother said gently, 'Darling, I know you love your presents, but you're starting to annoy everyone with them. You can sit down and have dinner with your birthday guests, but you have to promise me you won't talk about your watch or the perfume any more.'

Reluctantly the birthday girl agreed, and all through the meal she stuck to her promise, although she audibly sniffed her wrist every few minutes or so and dramatically kept raising her wrist to her ear to catch the sound of her new watch ticking. Despite her best efforts, no one asked what she was doing. Finally, in desperation, she blurted out, 'I'm not really supposed to say anything, but if someone hears or smells anything, it's me!'

DRIVING WITH MY FATHER

One day a father was out driving his car with his five-year-old daughter, Lou, and he beeped the car horn by mistake. Lou jumped and looked up at her dad, who said, 'Sorry, Lou, I did that by accident.'

Lou replied, 'I know you did, Daddy.'

'Oh? How did you know?'

'Because you didn't shout "IDIOT" afterwards.'

WHAT KIND OF GARDEN?

Megan Brown and her six-year-old daughter Bethany were sitting on their back patio when suddenly Megan had the bright idea that she wanted to dig up the paving stones and start a proper garden.

'But what sort of garden shall we have?' she asked her daughter. 'It would be nice to have a vegetable garden or would you prefer a flower garden with lots of colour?'

Quick as a flash, Bethany replied, 'We should plant a kindergarten.'

THE TRUTH AND NOTHING BUT

One mother tells a marvellous story in Nigel Rees's collection *Babes and Sucklings*, from when her son was two. He was sitting on his grandma's knee one day, playing with some beads that were round her neck, when he piped up, 'Ooh, a big fat tummy.'

Then there was a pause.

Then, 'Ooh, another big fat tummy!'

HURT FEELINGS

One afternoon Vicky Ferguson picked up her daughter Cate and her best friend Ashlin from nursery school. They were sitting in the back seat of the car chatting away happily. Half way home, however, they started to bicker and Cate suddenly shouted out, 'Mummy, Mummy, Ashlin just hurt my feelings.'

A furious Ashlin then responded, 'No, I did not! I'm sitting way over here.'

Father: Did you go to Anna's birthday party?

Daughter: No, I wasn't allowed. The invitation said 4-6. And I'm five.

TELEPHONE CHARGES

Anthony's mum was away one weekend at an important business conference. During a break, she decided to call home using reverse charges. Anthony, who was only six, picked up the phone and heard a stranger's voice say, 'We have your mother on the line. Will you accept the charges?'

Frantic, he dropped the phone and ran outside screaming, 'Daddy! Daddy! Someone's got Mummy! And they want money!'

FALSE TEETH

Heather used to work for a company who delivered 'meals-on-wheels' to the elderly, and decided to take her six-year-old daughter, Samantha, with her on her rounds for the day. Samantha was apparently intrigued by all the contraptions that the old people need to help them move about, such as Zimmer frames, walking sticks, electric stair lifts, wheelchairs, and so on. However, nothing could prepare her for when she spied a set of false teeth soaking in a glass of water. Thinking that her daughter was going to ask an embarrassing question to their owner, Heather braced herself.

'Oh, Mummy! Look at those,' pointed out Samantha excitedly. 'The tooth fairy won't believe it!'

THE LOGIC OF CHILDHOOD

On being taken to the ballet to see *Swan Lake* and noticing all the beautiful ballerinas dancing on tiptoe a little girl turned to her mother.

'Mummy,' she asked, 'why don't they just get taller dancers?'

CHARMING

Compliments can sometimes get lost in translation, especially where kids are involved. When Erika told her son he looked handsome, he replied, shocked, 'That's RUDE! How would you like it if someone called you a ham?'

If the tooth fairy is real then she must be really weird, otherwise why would she want to keep all those teeth? That's, like, really horrible!
   Martin — aged seven

ESCAPOLOGIST

One mother tells of the time when one of her cheeky sons was about five. He was such a naughty little boy that she sent him up to his room, telling him to remain there until he knew how to behave himself. Undaunted, he threatened to jump out of his bedroom window and escape. His mother warned him, 'If you jump out of your window you'll break your legs.'

To which her son replied, 'OK, well, I'll jump out yours then!'

WHITE WEDDING

It was eight-year-old Marion's first time at a wedding and she was very excited and full of questions. 'Mummy, why is the bride dressed all in white?' she asked her mother, who was sitting next to her.

'Because,' replied her mother, 'white is the colour of purity and happiness and today is the bride's happiest day.'

Marion thought about this for a while.

'So why is the bridegroom wearing black?'

SWIMMING LESSON

Professor John Pilkington Hudson tells the following story in the collection *Pass the Port Again*, which takes empirical logic to almost dangerous extremes. John and his wife were driving down a road by a canal and they stopped to give a lift to two boys who were camping further down on the bank. The canal looked deep, so they asked the boys whether they could swim.

One of them replied, 'We don't know because neither of us have fallen in yet.'

I was very good today. When they told me to sit on the naughty chair I sat on it without arguing!
Thomas — aged four

PLAY NICELY

One day Claire, aged six, asked her mother whether she could go outside to play in the play park with a group of boys. Her mother replied, 'I'm sorry, sweetheart, but no. Those boys are far too rough for you to go and play with.'

Claire thought for a while then asked, 'OK, but if I can find some smooth ones, can I play with them instead?'

HITTING THE BOTTLE

Debbie's five-year-old daughter, Beth, suffered from growing pains in her legs and had to take medicine prescribed by the family doctor. While her mother was brushing her teeth one morning, Beth found the right bottle in the bathroom cabinet and was trying, and failing, to open it herself.

Debbie told Beth she would have to open the bottle for her, and tried to explain that it was a childproof cap, which is why Beth couldn't get unscrew it.

Her daughter asked, eyes wide with wonder, 'But how does it know it's me?'

SEATBELTS REQUIRED

One hot summer evening, Barbara was driving back from a visit to friends with her two young children when a woman in a sports car ahead of them stood up and waved. She was stark naked.

As Barbara reeled from the shock, she heard her five-year-old daughter, Josie, shouting from the back seat, 'Mummy! That lady isn't wearing her seat belt!'

SOME THINGS JUST DON'T MOVE

On passing by a neighbour's house recently, John-Henry Pendle came across a little boy – who couldn't have been more than seven or eight years old – who was sobbing. When asked what the matter was he gulped back his tears and wiped his face.

'I've been digging this huge hole all afternoon,' he stuttered between sobs. 'It's taken me ages but Mum says I can't take it into the house.'

I like getting up in the morning and singing but Daddy always tells me to quieten down.
  Glen — aged eight

GOLF TEA ANYONE?

A father had planned a day of golf with some of his friends. While they waited for him in the car outside, getting more and more impatient, he desperately looked around for his bag of golf clubs.

'Where are my blasted golf tees?' he finally shouted out.

Suddenly his son came running into the room with a cup and a golf ball inside.

'Dad, Dad!' he shouted excitedly. 'It's all right, I've made you some golf tea!'

THEY'RE WATCHING YOU

One day Marcus was standing next to his Auntie Caroline, looking at a map in a shopping centre. There was a large arrow on the map with a statement printed underneath saying 'YOU ARE HERE'.

Marcus turned to his aunt and whispered suspiciously, 'How do they know?'

I'm glad I'm finally six! That's the oldest I've ever been my whole life!

Sam — aged six

I KNOW THE FEELING!

A mother was sitting with her young son in the reception area of her local doctors' surgery when a young woman pushed an elderly relative in a wheelchair into the room. As the young woman went to speak to the receptionist, the elderly man was left on his own.

Just as the mother was wondering if she should make small talk, her son walked up to the old man, patted his knee sympathetically and said, 'I know how you feel. My mummy sometimes makes me stay in the pram too.'

MANHUNT

The following exchange was recorded by Art Linkletter in *Kids Say the Darndest Things* and perfectly sums up how unintentionally truthful children can be.

Kid: My mother's busy looking everywhere for a man.

Linkletter: Where is the best chance to find one?

Kid: So far, it's best around Santa Monica, she says. But the trouble with most of them is that they yell, or drink or something.

Linkletter: That's too bad.

Kid: Oh, she doesn't give up easy. She had one a few weeks ago that was just about perfect except for two little things.

Linkletter: What were those?

Kid: He didn't like her. And he was already married.

KEEPING UP WITH THE NEWS

The following story once appeared in a church newsletter. A mother and father were arguing in the kitchen. Meanwhile, their six-year-old daughter was sitting at the kitchen table transfixed, her little head moving from left to right as she followed the gist of the debate. Her mother suddenly realized what they were doing, and immediately stopped talking and looked down at her daughter.

'I'm so sorry, sweetheart,' she said with a quiet smile, 'Mummy and Daddy shouldn't argue in front of you like that.'

'That's all right, Mummy', she said with a big smile. 'It's the only time I get to find out what's going on.'

THREE'S A CROWD

One grandfather, whose grandson had recently started school, contributed this anecdote to the collection *Little Gems*. After the boy's first week he came home and told his grandfather about his class. Apparently there were three brothers in his class with the same birthday and the teacher said this meant that they were called 'twiglets'.

Tell me when you're asleep, OK?
Damon — aged eight (to his brother)

RACING GRANNY

A grandmother was one day playing with her four-year-old grandson and his racing-car set. Later on, he was being naughty, and after three warnings, Granny very crossly told him to behave.

He came up to her with a long face, his head bowed down and lower lip trembling, and climbed into her lap to make peace.

'I still like you, Granny, but if you shout at me like that again, you might not be allowed to play with my racing cars any more.

DRIVING ME MENTAL

Vivien Womersley tells this story in *Babes and Sucklings* of the perspicacity of her four-year-old daughter when it came to navigation techniques. Her daughter was patiently sitting in the back of the car while Vivien drove and her husband map-read their way through a complicated German city.

Her husband became irritated when she turned left instead of right, but their daughter offered a practical solution: 'Daddy, why don't you drive and let Mummy shout at you.'

Is it called a supermarket because you buy soup there?
Jenny — aged four

SAY IT LIKE IT IS

When Ralph and Margaret Thompson had their grandchildren to stay one weekend, the children and Margaret woke up early and decided to make Ralph a morning cup of tea. Once he had woken up and had a sip, he made a fuss about how delicious it was, knowing that the kids had helped to make it.

Margaret replied that that was because it was made with love, but their three-year-old granddaughter exclaimed, 'No, it wasn't, Granny! It was made with water!'

A STONE'S THROW

A teacher overheard two boys talking earnestly together during the school break. The first boy said, 'My Dad can throw so far, he could hit that tree over there.'

The second boy went one further and claimed that his father could throw even further. 'He threw a stone right into the sky and up to Heaven.'

The first boy said, 'Ooh – did he hit God?'

The second boy, after a brief pause, replied, 'No, he wasn't at home.'

SNAP!

A mother was driving along while her two boys babbled away to one another on the back seat. The boys, one aged six and one eight, started reaching across the empty middle seat towards each other, saying 'Chomp! Chomp!' and clamping their arms together.

Mum, thinking war would soon break out, was about to tell them to keep their hands to themselves, when her younger son said, 'Chomp! I'm a Venus flytrap!'

The older son snapped back, 'Well, I'm a Jupiter flytrap. I'm much bigger!'

FAMILY TREASURES

One grandmother recalled a crafty afternoon with her eight-year-old granddaughter. They needed a pair of scissors for some cutting out and the nearest ones to hand were an antique filigree-handled pair that had been handed down through the family. The grandmother told her granddaughter she could use them but she had to be extremely careful as they were very special.

'Are they old?' she asked. Granny was pleased she seemed to be taking an interest in them and explained how she had been given them by her mother, who had been given them by her mother.

'Well, that explains it,' the granddaughter said.

'Explains what?'

'Why they don't work.'

HOW TO DRAW

The artist and art critic Roger Fry once asked a little girl he knew how she approached drawing and received a childishly wise response. The little girl replied, 'First I have a think, then I draw a line around it.' Artistic creation explained in a nutshell.

DEADLY SERIOUS

When he was a small boy, the poet and novelist Robert Graves, while saying his prayers one evening with his mother, asked her whether when she died she would leave him any money. 'If you left me as much as five pounds,' he said, 'I could buy a bicycle.'

'Surely you'd rather have me, Robby,' replied his rather concerned mother.

'But I could ride to your grave on it,' he reasoned.

LITTLE BOYS

Vernon, at the age of seven, got really lost one day while visiting a sports complex just outside Manchester. Seeing a ladies' changing room at the far end of a corridor he decided to go in and ask for help. However, when he opened the door and was spotted, he was suddenly overwhelmed by the sound of shrieking, as the naked women inside grabbed their towels and ran for cover.

Vernon watched the chaos in bewilderment and then asked, 'What's the matter, haven't you ever seen a little boy before?'

This is an octopus. It has eight testicles.
   Simon — aged seven

MIND YOUR MANNERS

This wonderful exchange from Shirley Trueman appeared in the *Daily Mail* letters section. During a visit to see her grandchildren, Daniel, aged seven, had given a sweet to his little sister Grace, aged two. Mother Rachel prompted Grace to remember her manners: 'And what do you say to Daniel?'

'More,' she replied.

Frankie (aged nine): Didier Drogba can't play in the world cup cos he was kicked in the tummy.

Mum: Who does he play for?

Frankie: Chelsea, England and the Irish Coast . . .

Mummy, I love you so much that when you die I want you to be buried outside my bedroom window.
Freddie — aged four

ASK A STUPID QUESTION

Children have a marvellous way of cutting straight through the guff and often giving very logical albeit incorrect answers. Viscount De L'Isle, Chairman of the Freedom Association, gave a wonderful example in *Pass the Port Again*: he had been speaking to a group of schoolchildren in a rural town in Western Australia and had quoted the Bible, saying, 'You are lucky to live in such beautiful countryside, truly "a land of milk and honey".'

'Where does that come from?' he asked a small girl.

'Cows and bees,' came the unhesitating reply.

For centuries, people thought the moon was made of green cheese. Then the astronauts found that the moon is really a big hard rock. That's what happens to cheese when you leave it out.
Donna — aged six

AND THE NOT SO LOGICAL

The following example of the occasional, well, madness of kids is taken from Art Linkletter's *Kids Say the Darndest Things* – and shows how strange the logic of children can be:

Linkletter: Anything exciting happen lately round your house?

Kid: Yes, I hit myself on the back of my head with a hammer.

Linkletter: That's too bad. How'd it happen?

Kid: I wanted to kill a fly.

Linkletter: Wait a minute. How could you see him if he was on the back of your head where the bump is?

Kid: He wasn't on the back of my head. He was on the table in front of me.

Linkletter: But I don't understand. Then why did you hit yourself on the back of the head with the hammer?

Kid: Silly! I wanted to smash him with my forehead!

PLAGUED BY DOUBT

Keith McFarland wrote into the *Daily Mail* with this gem, showing just how easily kids will consign you to history. He was discussing the 1665 Great Plague of London with his granddaughters, when Jessica, aged nine, questioned something he had said. Leaping to his defence, his younger granddaughter Mia, aged six, piped up, 'Don't argue with Grandad, he was there.'

Rainbows are just to look at, not really to understand.
Schoolchild — aged nine

WHEN I GROW UP

When you're small, everyone wants to know what you want to be when you grow up: the world is your oyster! But there are so many confusing options to consider in the world of work, which can look very different from the perspective of a child. Will you be an astronaut, a doctor, a fireman, an astrophysicist . . . or a squirrel? Sometimes the pressure to give an answer can just be too much.

Question to Billy, aged ten: What do your mother and father do for a living?

Billy: Mum's a lawyer but Dad just sits around a lot and wears wigs.

Question: Wigs?

Billy: Yes, he's a sort of . . . what do you call them? A sort of judge person.

DOCTOR, DOCTOR

A GP mother told this story about her four-year-old daughter. As she was driving to nursery school to drop her daughter off for the day, her little girl picked up the stethoscope that she'd left on the back seat. Her daughter seemed fascinated and began to play with it. The proud mother felt a surge of excitement as she briefly enjoyed the prospect that one day her darling girl might follow in her mother's footsteps. Then she spoke into the end of the stethoscope: 'Welcome to McDonald's! May I take your order?'

NOBLE PROFESSIONS

One mother wrote in *The Guardian* newspaper about a conversation she overheard between her eight-year-old son and a friend who were playing in the garden. When asked what his mother's job was, the little boy replied, 'She's a typist.' His mother's heart sank quietly. He was technically correct as his mother, Nobel Prize-winning author Nadine Gordimer, does indeed spend most of her days tapping away at a keyboard.

When I grow up I want to be a paperclip or a rubber band.
        Kelvin — aged nine

TRAFFIC JAM

The following exchanges took place between Art Linkletter, radio host and TV presenter, and his young interviewees and feature in his collection *Kids Say the Darndest Things*. Their views of the future are as yet a little hazy:

Linkletter: What do you want to be?

Kid: A traffic cop.

Linkletter: Ever see one close up?

Kid: I'll say! The other day Dad got a ticket for going through a stop sign and when the cop came up to the car I helped him. I told him that Dad hadn't been looking.

Linkletter: What do you want to be?
Kid: A nurse.
Linkletter: What if I came in with a broken arm?
Kid: I'd sew it on.
Linkletter: A broken head?
Kid: I'd sew it on.
Linkletter: Broken leg?
Kid: I'd sew it on.

When I grow up I want to be a shoe.
    Alice — aged seven

When I grow up I want to be just like my Daddy, but with some more hair.
    Kevin — aged eight

When I grow up I want to be the Queen so I can order everyone about and they will have to do what I say.
    David — aged six

SCHOOL PHOTOGRAPHS

One day, form teacher Miss Appleby was handing out copies of the school photograph while trying to tell her class how they should all go home and persuade their parents to buy one.

'Imagine,' she said, 'how much fun it will be when you're all grown up and can look back at this photo and say "There's Helen, she's a doctor now. And there's little Alan, he's a pilot these days . . ."'

Suddenly, a small voice at the back of the room piped up 'And there's Miss Appleby, she's dead and buried!'

I want to be a dinosaur doctor. To put dinosaurs back together.
    Edward — aged four

HOLLY GO LIGHTLY

When Dorothy Watt's granddaughter Holly, at the age of three and a half, decided she wanted to be a caterpillar, she spent three whole days shuffling around the house in a sleeping bag.

Mags, aged two: What's it say on my pyjama top, Mummy?

Mummy (getting carried away): It says 'Follow your dreams', Mags. It means that whatever you want to do in the future, you can do it. So it means that if you want to be a teacher or a doctor or anything when you grow up, you can do it.

Mags (excited): I can be ANYTHING!

Mummy: Yes, that's right, darling. So, what DO you want to be when you grow up?

Mags: A squirrel.

When I grow up I want to be an astronaut so I can get as far away from my little brother as possible.
    Sheila — aged nine

When I grow up I want to be an airline pilot because I'm not scared of heights.
    Schoolchild, Woking

POLICE FORCE

You can never rely on your children not to shop you, although you have to hope they don't do it on national television. Michael Barrymore once interviewed four-year-old Adam, a young contestant on *Kids Say the Funniest Things*, and got far more information than he bargained for:

Barrymore: What do you want to be when you grow up?

Adam: A policeman.

Barrymore: And have you got any handcuffs at all?

Adam: Some toy ones.

Barrymore: And has anyone else in the house got any handcuffs?

Adam: Me Dad.

FULL TIME JOB

One mother asked her son what he wanted to be when he was older. The answer came back, 'A mummy!' She had some difficulty in explaining to him that that was the one job he couldn't do, but he perked up when he decided he could be a sumo wrestler instead.

I want to be a penguin so that I can stay outside in the snow and slide on my tummy.
Nadine — aged four

WORKING DADS

In the following two excerpts from Art Linkletter's *Kids Say the Darndest Things* the children interviewed give a somewhat skewed perspective on their fathers' jobs:

Linkletter: So, your dad's a fireman. Does he tell you any exciting stories about big fires?

Kid: The most excitement is right at the fire station.

Linkletter: What happened there?

Kid: A fireman heard the bell, jumped out of bed, pulled on his pants, slid down the pole upside down, and knocked himself out when he hit the bottom.

Kid: My father's a nurseryman and raises flowers.

Linkletter: What sort?

Kid: Algerians.

Linkletter: Algerians?

Kid: Yes, red ones, white ones, pink ones.

Linkletter: Don't you mean geraniums?

Kid: Yes, Algerians.

When I grow up I'm going to find a boy my parents don't like and I'm going to marry him. That way I'll get back at them for all the times they've sent me to my room.

Katie — aged nine

SAWBONES

When Alex, aged five, appeared on the TV show *Kids Say the Funniest Things*, he was asked by Michael Barrymore what he wanted to be when he grew up. Alex replied, in what must have been a moment of equal pride and terror for his watching mother, 'I want to be a doctor so I can fix people and open them up and see how they work from the inside.

When I am a doctor I am going to open Mum up and check her bones and then stitch her back up again.'

When I grow up I want to be clever. I'm not very clever now although I can read. Perhaps I could do a job where I read to people? People who are stupider than I am.

Rowenna — aged nine

MULTITASKING

When Molly, aged five, was asked by her mother what she wanted to be when she grew up she said, 'A taxi driver!', but that was swiftly followed with 'An artist!', then 'A postman!' When told by her mum that she couldn't do all these jobs at once, she replied, 'Why not? I can do a different job each day.' Then she paused. 'I want to be a zoo keeper too.'

When I grow up I want to be a detective. Detectives get to wear really cool clothes and hunt people down and shoot them.
    Vernon — aged eleven

KNOW YOUR LIMITS

Belinda Grassick recently gave a lesson to a class of eight-year-olds during a school careers' day. She began by asking the children what they would like to be when they grew up. She asked one small boy called Trevor if he would like to be the Prime Minister.

'No,' said Trevor shaking his head. 'Absolutely not.'

'But why not?' Belinda asked, thinking that most children would love the idea of wielding so much power.

'I don't even know who's fighting who in our playground let alone in the world,' he replied sagely.

When I grow up I want to be a cooker.
      Schoolchild, Woking

When I grow up I want to be a teacher because you get really long summer holidays.
      Schoolchild, Woking

I never want to grow up. Grown-ups aren't allowed to play on the swings at the playground.
      Josh — aged six

BIBLIOGRAPHY

BOOKS

Adler, Bill (Editor), *Children's Letters to Santa Claus*, Century Books, 1994

Adler, Bill and Adler, Bill Jr. (Editors), *Kids' Letters to President Obama*, Ballantine Books, 2009

Brann, Christian (Editor), *Pass the Port Again*, Christian Brann Limited, 1980

Brann, Christian (Editor), *Pass the Port*, Christian Brann Limited, 1976

Casler, Mary Ann and Pearce Myers, Tona (Editors), *Butterfly Kisses: Gifts of Wisdom and Laughter from Our Children*, New World Library, 2001

Cosby, Bill, *Kids Say the Darndest Things*, Bantam Books, 1998

Fadiman, Clifton (Editor), *The Faber Book of Anecdotes*, Faber & Faber, 1985

Glavich, Mary Kathleen, *Catholic School Kids Say the Funniest Things*, Paulist Press, 2002

Hall, Donald (Editor), *The Oxford Book of American Literary Anecdotes*, Oxford University Press, 1981

Heller, David (Editor), *Dear God What Religion Were the Dinosaurs?: More Children's Letters to God*, Bantam Books, 1991

Hemple, Stuart and Marshall, Eric (Editors), *Children's Letters to God*, Kyle Cathie, 2006

John, Jory, *Thanks and Have Fun Running the Country: Kids' Letters to President Obama*, McSweeney's Publishing, 2009

Linkletter, Art, *Kids Say The Darndest Things!*, Celestial Arts, 2005

Lynas, Helen (Editor), *Out of the Mouths of Babes*, Andre Deutsch Limited, 1997

Minkoff, David, *The Ultimate Book of Jewish Jokes*, Robson Books, 2007

Phinn, Gervase, *Little Gems: Things Kids Say*, Dalesman Publishing Company Limited, 2004

Rees, Nigel, *Babes and Sucklings*, Unwin Paperbacks, 1983

Rees, Nigel, *The Cassell Dictionary of Anecdotes*, Weidenfeld & Nicolson, 1999

Rees, Nigel, *The Guinness Book of Humorous Anecdotes*, Guinness Publishing, 1994

Tibbals, Geoff (Editor), *Kids Say the Funniest Things* (Foreword by Michael Barrymore), Andre Deutsch Limited, 2000

Witwer Householder, Grace, *The Funny Things Kids Say Will Brighten Any Day*, Vanatech Press, 1995

NEWSPAPERS

Daily Mail

The Guardian

The Times

WEBSITES

There are hundreds of websites and blogs that were immensely helpful in compiling this book – too numerous to list in full – however I am grateful to the following sites which were particularly hilarious and helpful:

http://community.scholastic.com

http://fun.familyeducation.com

www.butchcrassidyjokes.com

www.butlerwebs.com

www.child-central.com

www.davesdaily.com

www.emmitsburg.net

www.grandparents.com

www.netfunny.com

www.rinkworks.com